To George,

Thanks for creating
an environment for
making this project
possible -

AL & Bob

THE ENTREPRENEUR

THE ENTREPRENEUR

Mainstream Views
and Radical Critiques

Robert F. Hébert
Albert N. Link

Foreword by
G. L. S. Shackle

PRAEGER SPECIAL STUDIES • PRAEGER SCIENTIFIC

Library of Congress Cataloging in Publication Data

Hébert, Robert F.
    The entrepreneur.

    Bibliography: p.
    Includes index.
    1. Entrepreneur — History. I. Link, Albert N.
II. Title.
HB615.H34   338'.04'09   81-21134
ISBN 0-03-059589-4   AACR2

Published in 1982 by Praeger Publishers
CBS Educational and Professional Publishing
A Division of CBS, Inc.
521 Fifth Avenue, New York, New York 10175 U.S.A.

© 1982 Praeger Publishers

23456789 145 987654321
Printed in the United States of America

for Diane and Carol

FOREWORD
G. L. S. Shackle

Can a list which begins with the dramatist, the symphonist, and the mathematician come naturally and fittingly at last to the business man, the entrepreneur? All of these are *originators*. The world which such a man senses around him may be in itself the same sort of world as presents itself to all of us. But what it means to him is different. It is for the *original mind* a sesame of untold riches of suggestion. All perception is no doubt an act of interpretation, of finding in, or injecting into sense-impressions a meaning, the collating with them of numberless memories of experience, the seeing in them of *possibilities*. This is in its own degree an act of origination. This same activity of thought, but at an enormously enriched, intensified and out-ranging degree, is what marks the creative writer, composer or theoretician, and it is what marks the entrepreneur.

The business man commands *resources*. Are these just material objects or collections, or money in the bank, or human colleagues with gifts of intellect and skill which they can offer as collaborators? All these things, even the skills, are in themselves *inert*. In themselves they are meaningless. It is when they are seen as means, as *potentiae*, as capable of uses, that they become resources. What is the indispensable psychic act which gives them meaning as resources? It is imagination, the ultimate creative act of thought in which men are tempted, with some excuse, to find their apotheosis, to see themselves as plenipotentiaries of divine power. Imagination is what informs the deeds of poet and symphonist, of the inventor of mathematics at the utmost limit of subtlety, of the sculptor and painter, and of the creator of a business. Yet this last exploit needs an extra gift. He must have nerve. He must commit himself,

vii

he must stake his chips. For no man can know what will be the sequel of his chosen act.

To admit that we do not know what will be the course of our affairs if we do this, or if we do that, goes somewhat against the grain. Yet if we claim that our choice of one course of action rather than another *makes a difference*, we are claiming that choice is an act of *absolute origination*, that it can have effects not implicit in antecedents. If so, there is no fore-knowing what a choice-to-come will be, by inference from its antecedents. Choices-to-come, made by ourselves or others, cannot be foreknown. Yet they will have effects, and they will affect to some greater or less degree the sequel of our present act. Then, in choosing that present act, we are in the nature of things in some respects blind. The entrepreneur is a man whose characteristic act is a gamble on his imagination. Of course, the business man uses reason and knowledge. He sees principles in the natural universe, he has insights into human powers and propensities. He can form judgements of what can come about, he cannot know uniquely what *will* come about.

What can his choice of action do? What can it do *in the present*, what difference can there be between one thought-commitment and another? One use of his resources will *exclude from possibility* some histories-to-come which in the abstract he can imagine. Another use of his resources will remove the obstacle, out impose one on some members of a different skein of imagined sequels. Let us then define enterprise. It is action in pursuit of the imagined, deemed possible. Any course of action must expose the chooser to numberless different sequels, rival hypotheses, some desired and some counter-desired. To say this is simply to say that freedom to create history entails unknowledge of what history will be created. The entrepreneur is a maker of history, but his guide in making it is his judgement of possibilities and not a calculation of certainties.

PREFACE

This book is a concerted effort to explore the relationship between entrepreneurship and economic activity. It is hoped that it will provide the conceptual framework, basic facts, and historical perspective essential to a better understanding of a highly important subject. Obviously, this slim volume cannot possibly treat such a complex topic in a comprehensive way. But the basic difficulty is not one of space; it is, rather, our still limited and imperfect grasp of a complicated human activity that recently was described by S. M. Kanbur as "the phenomenon which is most emphasized yet least understood by economists."

There is no surfeit of books and articles written on the nature and role of the entrepreneur in society. To date, however, the tendency has been to write historical case studies of individual "captains of industry" or to defend particular theories of entrepreneurial activity. The result is a lack of any singular notion of just who the entrepreneur is and what he does that makes him vital to the economic process. This book takes a different tack by presenting an intellectual history of the subject. By reviewing and examining what past and present minds have thought about entrepreneurs and entrepreneurship, we hope to build an interpretive framework that will help clarify and augment understanding of this elusive but critical notion in economic theory and practice.

We wish to thank a number of people whose efforts contributed to the conception and completion of this volume. Editor John Lambert of Praeger Publishers has been encouraging and cooperative from the outset. Professor William Breit of the University of Virginia expressed an early vote of confidence in the project and so fueled much of our enthusiasm to undertake it. Professor G. L. S. Shackle, who needs no introduction to the readers of this book, graciously and enthusiastically consented to write the foreword. He also followed the manuscript with interest, offering valuable suggestions and encouragement in the latter stages of its preparation. Bess Yellen and Delores Nuñez of the Manuscript Preparation Center in the School of Business at Auburn University provided peerless typing and editorial assistance with their usual quiet grace and efficiency. Some of the library research for the early chapters was provided by Katherine Graves, a graduate student in the Department of Economics at Auburn University. Our colleagues, Jürgen Backhaus and Roger Garrison, gave generously of their time to read parts of the manuscript, and each offered helpful comments and criticisms. Throughout it all, our wives offered the kind of firm support that made the whole task easier than it otherwise would have been. To all these people we are extremely grateful.

CONTENTS

CHAPTER 1

THE PLACE OF THE ENTREPRENEUR IN ECONOMICS

[T]he central idea of economics, even when its foundations alone are under discussion, must be that of living force and movement.

Alfred Marshall

OPENING STATEMENT

The theme of this book is the entrepreneur — his defining characteristics and his place in the economic order of things. At the outset, it appears that there are two alternative ways to approach this theme. One would be to ask what it is in the human condition, and particularly in the essential nature of business, that gives scope to a person possessing some special combination of talents, and what those talents are. Can a new business venture be imagined, designed in regard to its product and market, its technology and sources of finance, its required organization, special knowledge, and skills by any individual chosen at random? Is innovation (in the broadest sense) the province of every human agent? It would seem not. The complex,

1

exacting, and hazardous exploitation of conceived possibilities and seized opportunities requires an exceptional individual. If we elect to call him an entrepreneur the program for defining that term presents itself almost ready-made.

The other approach, the one we have elected to follow, is to examine the literature on the subject to see what meaning has been given to the term entrepreneur in the course of devising theories to deal with other questions and aspects of the economic world. By this second approach we have brought together, with commentary, interpretation, and occasional criticism, the thoughts of a score of minds on the question of the meaning and significance of entrepreneurship. The purpose of this chapter is to address some of the unanswered questions that surround the first approach before proceeding to the historical exegesis involved in the second.

WHO IS THE ENTREPRENEUR?

Entrepreneurship implies economic activity, and economics, as Ludwig von Mises informed us, is human action. Therefore two questions confront us immediately: What is it that makes man distinctly human? And, What is that combination of gifts that makes entrepreneurs stand out from the wider population? Both answers have a common root. The first question is problematic, and almost any answer given is likely to be controversial. The late Jacob Bronowski, who was highly respected in the scientific community, found the answer to man's uniqueness in his forward-looking imagination:

> There are many gifts that are unique in man; but at the centre of them all, the root from which all knowledge grows, lies the ability to draw conclusions from what we see to what we do not see, to move our minds through space and time, and to recognise ourselves in the past on the steps to the present. (1973, p. 56)

This definition is satisfying in a certain sense, but it nevertheless begs the more fundamental question of what it is in the human condition that gives prominence to this act of forward-looking imagination. A part of the answer to this last query must surely involve the concept of time and the nature of the constraint it places on individual choices. Every decision implies a present commitment to some future course of events. But it is the nature of time that we do not know what the future holds, no matter how much control we exert on the present. This is the sense of G. L. S. Shackle's statement in the foreword that "in choosing a present act we are in the nature of things in some respects blind." We are never completely blind, however. As Shackle also informs us, we have reason and knowledge. On the basis of reason and knowledge we can predict what consequences follow our present choices, but we can never know what they will be. Thus our choices are invariably accompanied by anticipation, which itself is an act of the imagination.

Epistemology, the study of the method and grounds of knowledge, is beyond the limited scope of our subject, but we nevertheless hold the view that regarding the creative process of discovery, the basic entrepreneurial act, there is little difference between the scientist and the businessman/entrepreneur. Apparent differences may exist in the motivation and/or the milieu of each class of actors. But consider the process of discovery alone for the moment. Those geniuses who have been responsible for the major innovations in the history of thought or in the world of affairs seem to have certain characteristics in common. One shared characteristic is skepticism, sometimes carried to the point of iconoclasm, in their attitudes to traditional ideas or ways of doing things. The other is an open-mindedness, often verging on naive credulity, toward new concepts and techniques. Out of this combination comes the capacity to perceive a familiar situation or problem in a new light. As Arthur Koestler (1959) has reminded us, the creative process is a wrenching away of a concept or technique from its traditional context or meaning. Over and over again, history has demonstrated this to be the case. Newton associated the fall of an apple not with its ripeness but with the motion of the moon. Henry Ford saw in the monotony of repetitive tasks the economic advantages of the assembly line and of mass production. The computer punch card had its prototype in the Jacquard loom. And so it has been throughout the history of the creative process.

Is it the function of the entrepreneur to create profit opportunities or merely to react to those opportunities that exist but have not yet been recognized? In the following chapters we shall see that both claims have been advanced. It would seem, however, that both kinds of behavior spring from the same center of imagination in the human psyche. Does it not take an act of forward-looking imagination to recognize a profit opportunity and act on it? Are not the same data received, interpreted, and acted upon differently by different individuals? How can we explain these differences? Are they not merely different powers of imagination?

Because we cannot know the future consequences of our present actions, each of us, as a decision maker, is placed at risk. As Shackle so aptly put it, the entrepreneur is a man whose characteristic act is a gamble on his imagination. Perhaps in this area the entrepreneur is different from the scientist, but if so, the difference is surely one of mere degree. The scientist usually stakes his chips in the form of his reputation, and in any event, all decisions involve commiting resources that have alternative uses, thereby incurring opportunity costs. Nevertheless, the ensuing historical exegesis will demonstrate that the position of risk in the theory of entrepreneurship is a matter on which past and present writers have shown little inclination to agree.

What, then, are the earmarks of the entrepreneur? What gifts of intellect, imagination, critical judgment, capacity for resolute action and sustained effort, courage, and detachment are required if a person is to bring novelty into the business scene and to shape in some degree its ongoing historical evolution? Is the continual and sometimes dramatic transformation of the means, ends, and methods of business the work of a type of moving spirit, a class of exceptional people? If so, what are they like, what precisely is exceptional in their psyches, their situations in life, their sources of inspiration? Finally, what sets their thoughts on fire and spurs them to action?

The answers to these questions form an ambitious research agenda that cannot be completed in so short a book as this. But the questions themselves provide a touchstone for the historical survey that follows. In this survey we shall see how the minds that shaped economic thought on the subject of the entrepreneur grappled or failed to come to grips with the questions we have posed. This survey thereby serves two purposes. It helps fill a void in the intellectual ancestry of a subject of vital importance to a dynamic economy, and it demonstrates in a most convincing way that the concept of entrepreneurship bids fair to the claim of being the most elusive concept within the purview of economics.

IMAGINATION, ENTREPRENEURSHIP, AND THE ECONOMIC PARADIGM

This study also serves an ancillary purpose that was originally no part of the authors' intention in setting out their plan of work. It raises, at least in indirect fashion, the question of what claim the idea of equilibrium has to dominate economists' thoughts and modes of analysis so pervasively. In a business world where dramatic success is so constantly the result of new knowledge, of discovery, invention, innovation, and all the activities that involve imagination, what is the relevance or supporting evidence of the supposition that history leads to a complete and comprehensive mutual adjustment of all rival interests? The purpose of the businessman/entrepreneur is to outwit his rivals, to destroy or to swallow them up. Can his achievement of purpose be characterized by a general equilibrium, the balancing of all conflicting interests?

Many economists find such questions heretical. Others find them futile, perhaps because the answers do not come easily. But as economists we would do well to remind ourselves that the equilibrium method came to economics through classical mechanics and that the physical principles that regulate the universe have been revised several times since that bygone era. To date few economists have tried to explore the implications for the social order of Boltzmann's entropy law, Heisenberg's uncertainty principle, or Einstein's theory of relativity. Do these principles have their analogs in the social order, as was assumed the case for classical mechanics in an earlier century?

We raise these provocative questions not because we have ready answers to them but because we cannot afford to ignore them indefinitely. The kind of environment in which the successful entrepreneur operates forces such questions upon us, however uncomfortable we may feel as a consequence. If the entrepreneur is a major force of change in the economic realm, if he is unique in the gifts he brings to the exercise of his peculiar function, if he deals in the unknowable consequences of his present and past actions, then as economists we should question the dominant mode of analysis that recognizes none of these attributes. Whether our understanding of the nature and significance of the entrepreneur in the social order has been helped or hindered by the dominance of the equilibrium paradigm is an open question. In order to answer that question it would seem necessary to have the historical record laid bare. In some small measure, the remainder of this book is devoted to that end.

CHAPTER 2

THE PREHISTORY OF ENTREPRENEURSHIP

[T]o study the entrepreneur is to study . . . the central figure in
economics.

A. H. Cole

BLANKNESS OF THE EARLY RECORD

The entrepreneurial function in society is probably as old
as the institutions of barter and exchange. Many economists
would probably agree with Arthur Cole's (1946) judgment that
a study of the entrepreneur is a study of the central figure in
economics. Yet despite his pivotal importance in economic
activity, the entrepreneur has been a shadowy and elusive figure
in the history of economic theory. Referred to often, but rarely
ever studied, the entrepreneur has wound his way through economic history, producing results often attributed to faceless
institutions or impersonal market structures.

This brief study raises two questions that must be answered
before research in entrepreneurship can be brought to a mature

state: First, quite bluntly, Who is the entrepreneur? And second, a corollary of the first, What does he do? Simple as these questions are, their answers are far from clear-cut. Indeed, there are almost as many definitions of entrepreneurship as there are students of the field. We have sought tentative answers to these questions in the annals of intellectual history. As an independent discipline, economics is hardly more than two centuries old. This makes it an elder statesman among the social sciences but a mere babe in the history of human activity. We therefore begin the search for understanding of entrepreneurship in the intellectual prehistory of economics.

The most striking thing about this early period is the blankness of its record on the nature of entrepreneurship. Traditionally, of course, entrepreneurship has been associated with the activities of businessmen. Without attempting to be very precise about the nature of entrepreneurship at this early stage of the study, it is incumbent upon us to take note of this rather long and conventional linkage.

MERCHANTS AND ADVENTURERS

Early economic thought was sensitive to the fact that economic activity is human activity and that acting agents can be roughly divided into two classes: those who lead and those who follow. Entrepreneurial talent, however ill-defined for the present, has always been closely aligned with the quality of leadership. The entrepreneur is generally held to be an active participant in the economic drama, and aside from royalty, was most likely to be found in early Western history among the ranks of merchants or the military. Military leaders especially qualified, because in this period of time wars were often begun for economic reasons. The general who designed and executed the necessary logistics and maneuvers pursuant to military victory bore considerable risk and stood to gain substantial economic benefits if he was successful.

Ancient merchants also exposed themselves and their possessions to risk in a way not unlike the military leader. Indeed, in early times the functions of trader and adventurer were merged in the same individual. Marco Polo, for example, was an adventurer seeking to establish important trade routes to the Orient. Less adventurous but no less important, merchants served as sedentary or mobile intermediaries of trade, with accompanying responsibilities and attendant risks. Each merchant customarily placed his possessions, and very often his life, at all manner of risks in the hope of obtaining a sizable reward. He was not, however, held in high esteem by the ancient philosophers. Aristotle, for one, recognized the place of the merchant in society but did not regard him as having a high calling. Indeed, he bore constant watching, lest society suffer from his overzealousness and rapaciousness. Said Aristotle:

> Of the two sorts of money-making one, . . . is a part of household management, the other is retail trade: the former necessary and honorable, the latter a kind of exchange which is justly censured; for it is unnatural, and a mode by which men gain from one another. (1924, p. 20)

Of course the Greek paranoia over maintenance of the status quo was partly a result of interpreting economic activity as a zero-sum game, an idea whose dominance persisted into the eighteenth century. By zero-sum game is meant a process whereby the gains to any one party or group of individuals are exactly offset by the losses to a second party or group of individuals. Greek and medieval philosophers tended to think that one man's gain (that is, profit) was another man's loss, so that trade did nothing to enhance the aggregate well-being of society.

Centuries of experience with markets should have taught us otherwise, but it is remarkable how persistent this idea is in contemporary society. Profit (the economic definition of which is the return to successful entrepreneurship) remains suspect in the minds of many well-educated people today, partly because of the long Western tradition of treating the businessman as bogeyman.

EARLY FORMS OF BUSINESS ORGANIZATION

The tendency to emphasize the importance of human decisions in the strategic nature of economic activity depends to a large extent upon the kind of business organization that prevails. In the ancient world, trade was on a relatively small scale. The link between the capitalist and the merchant adventurer depended on the contract they signed. The most common contract called for a loan from capitalist to merchant at the standard rate of 22.5 percent (including insurance). In such arrangements the capitalist was a passive risk bearer, whereas the merchant-adventurer exercised an active role in trade or commerce.

This type of institutional arrangement, known as the *societas maris*, persisted in commercial societies for many centuries. In Venice, Europe's most active trading society in the thirteenth century, the same business organization became formalized in the *colleganza*, a cooperative arrangement between a traveling and an investing partner. The terms, however, were less generous to the Venetian entrepreneur than to his ancient counterpart. Raymond de Roover (1963a) noted that while the investor provided capital for the venture and took the financial risk, the traveling partner embarked on a hazardous sea voyage, handled the actual business, and took the personal risk of losing his life or at least of enduring all of the discomforts involved. But when it came to sharing the profits, the capitalist received the lion's share of three-fourths, while the entrepreneur-manager received only one-fourth. De Roover speculated that the capitalist received a higher return because "life was cheap and capital scarce" (1963a, p. 49), but Fritz Redlich (1966) found the explanation instead in the medieval prohibition of usury. The medieval adventurer, unlike his ancient counterpart, was enjoined from simply borrowing the capital he needed and paying a fair interest thereon. The Church forced him into forming a partnership with a capitalist, and by virtue of its attitude toward usury, gave undue weight to the latter.

This last explanation, however, overlooks the fact that the medieval doctrine of usury was derived from the ancient Greek invectives against interest taking. Aristotle's was a major voice in this respect that echoed through the teachings of the Church Fathers. Of course, the authority of the Church may have made the difference between an effective prohibition in the Middle Ages and a philosophical injunction in the Hellenic era. The salient points, however, are that the merchant-adventurer was a commonplace of ancient and medieval societies and that he tended to fare better or worse, economically speaking, as a result of the success he had in overcoming risk or legal/institutional constraints or both.

PROPERTY RIGHTS AND THE ENTREPRENEURIAL FUNCTION

One manifestation of entrepreneurship involving risk bearing and initiative is the occupation of tax farmer. A tax farmer is one who bids for the exclusive right to collect taxes in the name of the Crown. The amount of each bid is related in a predictable way to the bidder's evaluation of the amount of taxes he can collect. The advantage to the monarch who farms out the collection of taxes is that he knows his revenues and receives them in advance. The risk to the tax farmer is simply this: If he fails to collect in taxes the amount bid for his exclusive right, he suffers a financial loss to the extent of the difference. Conversely, of course, if he collects more than the amount of his bid, the difference is his to keep. The practice of tax farming can be traced back as far as ancient Greece and may, upon closer investigation, be found to be even older.

One of the interesting things about tax farming is that its practice helps explain how property rights ownership and the security of these rights impinge on the behavior of entrepreneurs. As economic agent, the incentive that spurs the entrepreneur to action is the opportunity to obtain profit. But making profit, while a necessary condition, is not a sufficient condition for entrepreneurial activity. The entrepreneur must also be reasonably assured that he may keep entrepreneurial profits that he legitimately acquires. Thus certain institutional practices in a market economy will tend to encourage a high level of entrepreneurial activity, especially (1) a free and open economy that permits equal access to entrepreneurial opportunities, (2) guarantees of ownership in property legally acquired, and (3) stability of institutional practices that establish points 1 and 2.

It may be that the prevalence and longevity of tax farming as an entrepreneurial activity were due to the relatively greater security enjoyed by the fiscal entrepreneur as against the merchant-adventurer, whose goods were subject to fire, theft, storm, and other destruction and whose profit did not always reflect his diligence in supervision or management.

THE EVOLUTION OF A CONCEPT

Redlich has astutely observed that in the model of a business enterprise the provision of capital and management and strategic decision making (entrepreneurship) all "stand on the same level; none can be thought away without distorting reality to the point of no return. On the other hand, when we look at individual enterprises in specific situations any one of these three functions may temporarily become 'primary' " (1966, p. 715). Whether or not one agrees with this assessment, it shall become obvious in the ensuing chapters that what usually vies for supremacy in economic analysis is one theory of entrepreneurship or another, each emphasizing different critical aspects of the "entrepreneurial" function. Historically, the risk-bearing function of entrepreneurship became less important after the establishment of limited liability and its attendant new forms of business organization. Later, innovation came to be stressed more than other aspects of entrepreneurship in theories of economic growth. The third wave of entrepreneurial theories, in turn, seemed to stress the importance of perception and adjustment in an equilibrating framework.

The term entrepreneur does not appear often in the prehistory of economics. It is a word of French origin that first made an obtrusive appearance in the writing of Richard Cantillon, an eighteenth-century businessman and financier who is the subject of the next chapter. Cantillon is significant in this connection not merely because he used the term but because he infused it with precise economic content and gave the concept analytic prominence. The fact that common, though imprecise, usage of the term existed prior to Cantillon is corroborated by an entry in Savary's *Dictionaire Universel de Commerce* (Paris, 1723) in which "entrepreneur" is defined as one who undertakes a project; a manufacturer; a master builder. An earlier form of the word, "entreprendeur," appears as early as the fourteenth century (Hoselitz 1960). Throughout the sixteenth and seventeenth centuries the most frequent usage of the term connoted a government contractor, usually of military fortifications or public works.

One economist who has extensively researched the history of entrepreneurship has shed considerable light on the early evolution of the concept. Bert Hoselitz notes that the typical entrepreneur of the Middle Ages, usually a cleric, was "the man in charge of the great architectural works: castles and fortifications, public buildings, abbeys and cathedrals" (1960, p. 237). Until the end of the twelfth century, the functions of inventor, planner, architect, builder, manager, employer, and supervisor were all combined in the notion of an "entrepreneur," but risk bearing and capital provision were not part of the concept. As capitalism began to push aside the vestiges of feudalism, a clearer distinction emerged between the one who performed artistic and technical functions and the one who undertook the commercial aspects of a great task. Cantillon's work is a watershed in the development of entrepreneurial theory precisely because by the time we get to his treatment of the subject, emphasis is being placed squarely on the purely commercial aspects of "getting things done" in a market economy.

CHAPTER 3

THE FIRST STEPS
ON A NEW PATH

Many people set themselves up . . . as merchants or entrepreneurs
. . .: they pay a certain price for produce depending on where
they purchase it, to resell wholesale or retail at an uncertain
price.

Richard Cantillon

RICHARD CANTILLON

The first important work in economics that gave the entrepreneur a central role in trade was Cantillon's *Essai sur la
nature du commerce en général*, published in 1755, 21 years
after the author's death. Few individuals in the history of
economics are more shrouded in mystery than Cantillon
(1680?-1734). He was of Irish extraction, but the exact year of
his birth has never been settled, and he is often confused with
a relative of the same name. Other prominent facts of his life
are historically muddled, and those activities of which he did

partake were controversial in his lifetime. Even Cantillon's death was sensational, insofar as he was murdered by an angry servant whom he had discharged a few days earlier.

Cantillon made his fortune in Paris as a banker who gained at the expense of John Law's infamous inflationary scheme that historians know as the Mississippi Bubble. The ingenuity with which he saw through and profited from Law's "system" is itself a demonstration of considerable entrepreneurial skill. In fact, Law and Cantillon both personify the characteristics we have come to identify with a certain type of entrepreneur: foresight, skill, daring, and purposive action.

Law obtained permission from France's prince regent in 1716 to establish a royal bank, and shortly thereafter he secured an exclusive franchise to form a trading company in the New World that was popularly known as the Mississippi Company. The company soon won a monopoly of French foreign trade and thereafter began to assume the French government debt by trading shares of the company's stock for certificates of indebtedness. With the certificates came the exclusive right to collect certain taxes. Promises of large dividends to investors pushed share prices up sharply, and a frenzy of stock speculation ensued. The system ultimately ended when stock values rose out of all proportion to the real value of the company's assets, and in 1720, the bubble burst.

Cantillon accurately foresaw the complete course of Law's scheme and made a great deal of money by liquidating his Mississippi holdings at the peak of the speculative boom. He reinvested the proceeds in Britain and Holland, at the same time feeding the British mania for speculation by advancing funds to English speculators who bought Mississippi shares that they subsequently pledged as security for their loans. Cantillon shrewdly sold this collateral before the price of the stock broke, thus pocketing speculative profits in addition to interest on the loans he had made. His practice provoked numerous lawsuits by his borrowers, but Cantillon successfully defended himself against all claims.

As one of the few men to see through, and profit from, Law's gradiose scheme, Cantillon earned a place in history. But his contributions to economic theory provide a far better epitaph. Among those contributions was, to all appearances, the first economic theory of entrepreneurship.

ENTREPRENEURS AND THE MARKET SYSTEM

Cantillon's historic *Essai* makes over a hundred references to the entrepreneur as a pivotal figure who operates within a set of economic markets. It is important to note the difference between a "market" and a "marketplace." To the economist, the market is a mechanism that produces prices, that is, a specific institution with its own rules upon which a powerful analytic structure can be (and has been) built. But to the historian, "market" often means a meeting place for the transfer of goods from one party to another. This kind of marketplace is not necessarily the basis of the economic theory that economists have created. In fact, markets as places of exchange existed long before the emergence of markets in the more specialized sense (Neale 1957).

Cantillon's vision of the market was that of a self-regulating network of reciprocal exchange arrangements. His markets produced (equilibrium) prices, and the entrepreneur had a central role in effecting this result. In this sense, Cantillon's vision was remarkably modern, a point that has been emphasized by J. J. Spengler (1960). The parts that make up this system — custom, law, trade relations — evolve over time in response to "need and necessity," which in turn bind all the inhabitants together into reciprocal arrangements. The driving force of this system is self-interest, which is manifest most prominently, although not exclusively, by the actions of a class of entrepreneurs who are responsible, in Cantillon's words, for "all the exchange and circulation of the State" (1931, p. 56). Considering the period in which Cantillon wrote, it is somewhat surprising that the entrepreneur was not fit neatly into a particular social hierarchy. On the contrary, Cantillon almost made social standing irrelevant to entrepreneurship. What he did consider relevant was the function, not the personality, of the entrepreneur. Cantillon was perfectly willing to admit that "even beggars and robbers are . . . entrepreneurs," providing they take chances, that is, face uncertainty (1931, p. 55). Moreover, being an entrepreneur does not exclude one from being something else. Indeed, entrepreneurs are linked in reciprocal trade arrangements with other market participants and therefore "become consumers and customers one in regard to the other" (1931, p. 53).

Cantillon's theory suggests that an entrepreneur is someone who has the foresight and willingness to assume risk and takes the action requisite to making a profit (or loss). This self-interested (and daring) activity has important social consequences, insofar as it is the actions of entrepreneurs reacting to price movements (that is, profit opportunities) that continuously serve to bring about a (tentative) balance between supplies and demands in specific markets. The notion that the entrepreneur is an equilibrating mechanism in a market economy originally came from the insightful mind of Cantillon.

UNCERTAINTY AND RISK

The earliest use of the term entrepreneur did not include risk bearing and capital provision among his duties. Cantillon, however, originated the theory of the entrepreneur as risk taker and, in so doing, set the theory of entrepreneurship on a new course. What he discovered for himself was that disregarding the "Prince" and the landlords, the whole population could be divided into two classes, entrepreneurs and those otherwise engaged in economic activity. The former were distinguished by the fact that their incomes were uncertain; the latter by the fact that their incomes were known and (contractually) fixed. Cantillon was impressed by the fact that gainfully employed people such as farmers, craftsmen, wholesalers, retailers, innkeepers, tailors, and others "buy at a certain price and sell at an uncertain price" (1931, p. 51). Thus they operate at risk. For Cantillon, risk is inherent in the nature of any trade that is ruled by competition, so there is literally no way to separate the concepts of competition and entrepreneurship in his theory: One is a consequence of the other.

The enterprise that seemed to illustrate best the inherent risks of entrepreneurship was that of the farmer:

> The farmer is an *entrepreneur* who promises to pay to the land-owner, for his farm or land, a fixed sum of money . . . without assurance of the profit he will derive from this enterprise. He employs part of the land to feed flocks, produce corn, wine, hay, etc. according to his judgement without being able to foresee which of these will pay best. The price of these products will depend partly on the weather, partly on the demand; if corn is abundant relatively to consumption it will be dirt cheap, if there is scarcity it will be dear. Who can foresee the number of births and deaths of the people in a state in the course of the year? Who can foresee the increase or reduction of expense which may come about in the families? And yet the price of the farmer's produce depends naturally upon these unforeseen circumstances, and consequently he conducts the enterprise of his farm at an uncertainty. (Cantillon 1931, p. 49)

Cantillon's explanation of the entrepreneur's role has a distinct supply-side emphasis. He does not so much see the entrepreneur as creating demand through new production or merchandising techniques; rather, he sees him providing the right goods at the right place in order to satisfy preordained consumer wishes. Thus Cantillon's entrepreneur must be forward-looking, but he need not be innovative in the strict sense of the term. He must, however, be alert, for when particular supplies and demands do not match, it is the entrepreneur who springs into action.

The producer-entrepreneur's response to a profit opportunity involves a change in production. However, other entrepreneurs engage in arbitrage. Thus Cantillon argued that if price differences persist between Paris and the countryside, then

> entrepreneurs . . . will buy at a low price the products of the villages and will transport them to the Capital to be sold there at a higher price; and this price difference will of necessity pay for the upkeep of the horses and drivers, as well as the profit of the entrepreneur, without which he would terminate his enterprise. (1931, pp. 150-52)

Even a pure arbitrage action such as the one described in this passage involves some risk, although Cantillon did not belabor the point. The arbitrageur can perceive that a product sells for one price at one place and at a higher price somewhere else; but if he buys in the first to sell in the second, he must be careful. The transactions are not instantaneous, and something might occur in the interim to change seemingly certain profits into losses.

Although we are hard-pressed to attribute to Cantillon — or any early economist — a full-blown theory of profit, it is nevertheless interesting to note in the last part of the material just quoted that Cantillon recognized the legitimacy of entrepreneurial profits and indeed the necessity of profits in order that the economic function of the entrepreneur be performed. Early economists who followed Cantillon's lead were therefore clearly under no delusions that profit was a dirty word.

CAPITAL AND ENTREPRENEURSHIP

One of the perpetual points of contention in competing theories of entrepreneurship is to what extent the roles of entrepreneur and capitalist can be separated. Specifically, does a risk-bearing theory of entrepreneurship require that an entrepreneur own certain capital assets that are ipso facto the "stakes" in the profit/loss game? The most consistent picture of the entrepreneur that emerges from Cantillon's writings is, as already noted, one who faces uncertainty and bears its associated economic risks. This seemingly requires that entrepreneurs own certain assets or have access to certain assets through credit arrangements. How else can an entrepreneur be meaningfully exposed to risk? If one has nothing to lose, then there can be no such thing as a loss. And a theory of entrepreneurship that explains gains but does not allow for losses is evidently one-sided. Cantillon did not confront this issue directly, but the strongest textual evidence suggests that his entrepreneur is a capitalist, even if to a very limited extent. He need not be a capitalist in the strict, pecuniary sense, however. Cantillon included doctors, lawyers, and other professionals (even beggars and robbers) as "entrepreneurs of their own labor," which takes us very close to the modern concept of human capital. All that is needed to bring his idea up to date by contemporary standards is to recognize that even the penniless entrepreneur incurs potential losses to the extent that he faces opportunity costs of his time and talents.

This last point is an important one, which has been clarified recently by Kanbur (1980). Consider an individual with no means of his own. Suppose he foresees an opportunity that promises an uncertain rate of return, and he borrows capital at a fixed, contráctual rate of interest. If the enterprise does so badly that the borrower cannot repay the contracted amount of principle and interest, the financial loss falls solely on the lender, as the borrower has no means of his own. But as Kanbur argues:

> Surely the gains and losses, and hence risks, are to be thought of as being relative to the opportunity cost of the enterprise. For example, it could be that the prospective entrepreneur has open to him a safe return in an alternative occupation. *Relative* to this return, the contract above does indeed present our entrepreneur with the possibility of losses — he *could* end up worse than if he had taken up a safe occupation, though of course he will always end up better than if he had taken up no occupation at all. This is the sense in which the prospective entrepreneur faces risks. . . . (1980, p. 493)

For the man of means who foresees an uncertain opportunity, the problem remains of how to separate his risk-bearing role as capitalist from his risk-bearing role as entrepreneur. Conceptually, it is possible to do this, but we must look for a working model in the form of the *colleganza* of 13th century Venice or in the earlier *societas maris* of ancient Greece. It will be recalled that in these arrangements the functions of capitalist and entrepreneur were separate; the former was an investing partner and the latter a traveling/managing partner. It should be expected that the opportunity cost of the capital in such an arrangement will be different from the opportunity cost of the entrepreneurial effort, and it is in proportion to these different costs that the respective risks have to be conceptualized and, ultimately, measured.

The marketplace has of course provided a mechanism, in the form of insurance, whereby an entrepreneur can shift some of the risks he might otherwise face to another party who is willing to bear it for an appropriate reward. However, insurance and its impact on entrepreneurial effort were beyond the pale of Cantillon's discussion. We shall have reason to take up this idea again (see Chapter 6). For now, we merely suggest that perfect insurance of risk is unlikely because of the problems of moral hazard and adverse selection (Rothschild and Stiglitz 1976).

A HARBINGER OF THE FUTURE

Cantillon argued that the origin of entrepreneurship lies in the lack of foresight individuals have with regard to the future. It is noteworthy that he did not consider this lack of foresight a defect of the market system; he accepted it as part of the human condition. Uncertainty is a pervasive fact of everyday life, and those who must deal with it continuously in their economic pursuits are entrepreneurs. For Cantillon, it is the function of the entrepreneur, not his personality, that is therefore of critical importance to economic analysis. This function is at the heart of Cantillon's conception of a market system; indeed, without it, the system as we know it does not operate.

William Stanley Jevons (1931), an important economist in his own right, described Cantillon's *Essai* as "the cradle of political economy." Other writers have judged Jevons' praise effusive, but whatever its general merits, at least on the subject of the entrepreneur, Cantillon was a harbinger of the future. He not only provided the first formal statement of the entrepreneur's role and significance in the market economy but also developed one of the most enduring concepts of the entrepreneur.

Despite his pioneer efforts in the theory of entrepreneurship, however, Cantillon's conception was myopic in one important respect. It excluded the "Prince," the landlords, and certain laborers from uncertainty. The landlords, Cantillon argued, received rents that were fixed by contract and by custom (generally supposed to be equal in value to one third of the produce). Common laborers, too, received wages under similar institutional arrangements. Thus the incomes of these groups were viewed as certain. But surely Mises was correct when he asserted that "no proprietor of any means of production, whether they are represented in tangible goods or in money, remains untouched by the uncertainty of the future" (1963, p. 253). Cantillon's vision of entrepreneurship needed to be widened, and was, first by Frank Knight and then again by Mises. But that is another story, which will be told further on.

CHAPTER 4

A FORK IN
THE ROAD

[The entrepreneur] estimates needs and above all the means to satisfy them.

J. B. Say

Cantillon's work enjoyed considerable popularity in France, circulating freely in manuscript form for two decades before its publication. But no French writer on economics produced anything of the caliber of Cantillon's *Essai* until François Quesnay (1694-1774), founder of the physiocratic school, made his mark on economics in 1758. Among French writers, the distinction between capitalist and entrepreneur was common until the physiocrats introduced new shades of meaning to the term. To a large extent, customary usage may have reflected business practice, for a common form of French business organization in the eighteenth and nineteenth centuries was the *commandite*, in which a "sleeping" partner provided capital, and the active partner was the entrepreneur (Taymans 1949). Thus in a fundamental sense, the *commandite* was akin

23

to the *colleganza* of the thirteenth century and the earlier *societas maris* of the pre-Christian era.

FRANÇOIS QUESNAY

Quesnay entered economics in his sixties, after enjoying considerable success as a physician and an author of books on medicine, biology, and philosophy. His renown as a physician brought him to the court of Louis XIV, where he personally attended Madame du Pompadour. In economics, his fame rests on his pioneer contributions to national income analysis and his acknowledged leadership of the first school of economic thought, physiocracy — the term refers to those (physiocrats) who believe in a rule of nature. Quesnay's ability to win a following during a short span of time derived in part from his power and influence in high places, in part from his attractive personality, and in large measure from the substance of his message. Our intent here is not to review the whole range of physiocratic thought but to focus on its use of the term entrepreneurship.

Quesnay's analytic system was grounded in agrarian capitalism. It was a system that featured three economic classes whose part in the economy was related to, and determined by, the economic function of its members. A proprietary class owned the property rights in land that it leased to the productive class (farmers), who in turn produced the raw materials demanded by a sterile class of artisans. The unique feature of the system is that agriculture appeared as the only sector capable of producing a net product. Landlord-proprietors advance capital to the enterprising farmers, who in turn produce agricultural commodities, the value of which exceeds the explicit costs of production. That surplus value is claimed by the proprietors in the form of rent; and in each subsequent period, the process is repeated in the same fashion.

This paradigm, which is the core of physiocratic macroanalysis, presents a picture of a static society in which no accumulation of capital occurs and no uncertainty is present. The same gross product is produced year after year, and the same distributive share repeatedly goes to each of the three economic classes. Hence the capital advances are equal and certain each year and so are the payments to the farmers who performed the entrepreneurial function.

In this static version of the theory there is no sense in which Quesnay could have developed a theory of entrepreneurship more advanced than Cantillon's. Quesnay, in fact, did not use the term entrepreneur in any technical sense; he merely employed it in the connotation it had acquired during the second half of the eighteenth century. Quesnay repeatedly referred to the operator of a large farm as an entrepreneur "who guides and turns to his account his enterprise by his intelligence and his wealth" (1888, pp. 218-19). Thus it appeared that the entrepreneur was a mere patron who supervised the labor process but did not participate in it directly. The property rights of this entrepreneur were attenuated, moreover, because of the physiocratic distinction between proprietors and farmers. For these reasons, Quesnay's notion of the entrepreneur was not particularly robust.

NICOLAS BAUDEAU

It was not Quesnay but his followers who developed a theory of entrepreneurship that contained many modern elements. The first of these physiocrats who helped advance the theory of entrepreneurship was a clergyman, Abbé Nicolas Baudeau (1730-1792), who began as a foe of physiocracy but later converted to the French doctor's creed. What Baudeau did was to place the agricultural entrepreneur in essentially the same position as Cantillon's risk bearer, then take the concept one step farther. This involved, at least implicitly, moving outside the static conception of the economy envisioned by Quesnay.

Baudeau's entrepreneur is clearly motivated by profits. He is a decision-making individual who bears risk because of the nature of his activities, but he also invents or innovates in order to reduce his costs and thereby raise his profit. This second feature of entrepreneurship represents an advance over

Cantillon's theory, becoming more important, as we shall see, at a later stage of the development of the theory of entrepreneurship. But more central to our present concern is the nature of risk faced by the agricultural entrepreneur. In a purely physical sense, rent in the physiocratic economy was the surplus of agricultural value over necessary costs of production. But from the standpoint of the individual farmer-entrepreneur, rent was a cost determined in advance of production. The physiocrats favored stabilizing these costs as much as possible through long-term leases, yet wage rates were considered fixed at or near the level of subsistence. Hence, on the one hand, the farmer-entrepreneur operating with a long-term lease faced a very rigid cost structure. But, on the other hand, the price of his crop was uncertain, as was the actual outcome of the harvest. Such uncertainty put the entrepreneur in precisely the same position Cantillon had placed him, facing certain expenses and uncertain revenues.

Where Baudeau went beyond Cantillon is in emphasizing and analyzing the significance of ability. Baudeau underscored the importance of "intelligence" — the entrepreneur's need for knowledge and information. Because the agricultural entrepreneur carries on production at his own risk for his own account, he must have the capacity to act in an entrepreneurial way; that is, he must be able to exercise control over productive processes. Failing this, the entrepreneur would be a mere pawn in the capitalist game. Baudeau thought otherwise: "Such is the goal of the grand productive enterprises; first to increase the harvest by two, three, four, ten times if possible; secondly to reduce the amount of labor employed and so reduce costs by a half, a third, a fourth, or a tenth, whatever possible" (1910, p. 46). In order to do this the entrepreneur had to be an innovator, and Baudeau was fully alert to the progress that invention makes possible.

Physiocratic writings are replete with proposals to improve agricultural techniques, many of which were oriented toward the upgrading of human capital or the dissemination of better information. Hoselitz (1960, pp. 246-27) has uncovered several proposals: translation of English texts on agriculture; nationwide distribution of handbooks and guides describing new tools, crops, or procedures; prizes; honors; agricultural research; model farms; and pilot plants. There was a confidence that when the right knowledge became available, these innovations would be adopted by alert entrepreneurs, spurred to action by the opportunity for profit. In this early fashion, then, the entrepreneur as innovator appeared in economic literature.

Baudeau's theory of entrepreneurship presupposes that events impinging on economic activity tend to fall into two categories: those that are subject to human control and those that are not. To the extent that the entrepreneur confronts the former, his success will depend on his knowledge and ability; to the extent that he confronts the latter, he places himself at risk. Seen in this light, his theory of entrepreneurship is more general than Cantillon's, which concentrated exclusively on the risk aspects of entrepreneurial activities.

ANNE-ROBERT JACQUES TURGOT

Anne-Robert Jacques Turgot's (1727-1781) place in history is assured by his long and distinguished administrative career in French government, culminating in his service from 1774 to 1776 as finance minister to Louis XIV. Born into an old and well-placed Norman family, Turgot grew into an extremely gifted and precocious young man who was more interested in becoming a polymath than a specialist in any one endeavor. One of his many gifts was lucid exposition in the field of economics, and although he resisted the label of economist (Meek 1973), his chief accomplishment as a writer was in mapping out the theory of an entrepreneurial economy.

Turgot's ideas did not coincide at all points with those of physiocracy; nevertheless he was on good terms with the members of Quesnay's inner circle. Moreover, he was fully in tune with the central feature of Quesnay's analysis, the concept of "advances" (that is, capital) and its use as a basis for an explanation of the economic mechanism. The important difference between Quesnay and Turgot is that Turgot went farther than Quesnay in two vital respects: He saw capital as the basis for an explanation of the entire economy, not solely the agricultural sector, and he added the idea that the profit of the entrepreneur who makes these "advances" is part of the absolutely necessary expenses of production. By 1766, Turgot was clearly expounding the existence and crucial importance of an entrepreneurial class.

For our study it is instructive to compare Cantillon and Turgot on the subject of the entrepreneur. Turgot may have learned much from Cantillon, but the true nature of their affiliation has never been made historically precise. Both men placed the entrepreneur at the heart of the market system, although the characteristics of this central human force were different for each writer. Capital, in the pecuniary sense, was not a prerequisite of Cantillon's entrepreneur. We saw in the last chapter that he identified many individuals as entrepreneurs of their own labor without any capital, such as chimney sweeps, water carriers, even beggars and robbers. This class of operators was only occasionally prominent, usually working behind the scenes to facilitate the establishment of market equilibrium by production or arbitrage. By contrast, Turgot assumed the entrepreneur to be a wealthy man who employed labor in a productive process either in agriculture or in manufacturing. Independent workmen and artisans were thereby excluded from this category. The critical element in Turgot's theory was the motive force of "advances" by the entrepreneur in the productive process. In practice and in theory, Turgot did not distinguish between "capitalist" and "entrepreneur." The same individual drove the engine of his economic theory, namely, the capitalist-entrepreneur who supplied the capital and employed the laborers that made production possible.

Meek (1973) has argued that Cantillon was analyzing a society in which the capitalist-entrepreneur was just beginning to separate himself out of the ranks of independent workmen, whereas Turgot was analyzing an economy in which this process had been completed and in which the capitalist system had consolidated itself in all fields of economic activity. In his *Reflections on the Formation and Distribution of Wealth* (1766), Turgot presented a clear picture of an economy in which capitalism embraces all spheres of production. In this description the "industrious" classes are divided into entrepreneurs and hired workers (with a sharp differentiation between the profit of the former and the wage of the latter), free competition is widespread and monopoly nonexistent, landownership appears as little more than another form of investment of capital, and a general glut of goods is impossible because savings are transformed immediately into investment. What is missing, however, is any built-in specification about technological progress, any hint that the entrepreneur is an innovator or anything more than a capitalist, or any critical emphasis on the dynamic rather than the static aspects of the economy.

It is also instructive to compare, however briefly, Turgot's vision of the entrepreneur with Quesnay's and Baudeau's. Although Quesnay did not elaborate a complete theory of entrepreneurship, his description of the entrepreneur as one who supervises and produces value by his intelligence and his wealth contains an abundance of hidden meaning that served as a point of departure for both Baudeau and Turgot. Baudeau remained closer to Quesnay insofar as his entrepreneur is a farm operator who plans, organizes, and takes risks and is a wealthy man. Turgot's entrepreneur is a rich merchant or industrialist who advances capital and plans or supervises productive activity in an effort to accumulate more wealth. It is significant that Baudeau added innovation to the purview of the entrepreneur and Turgot did not, although it would be wrong to exaggerate the differences between these two, as, in the final analysis, they both swam in the same current.

Hoselitz (1960) has placed Turgot's theory of entrepreneurship midway between the traditional French view, which holds the entrepreneur to be chiefly a risk bearer (Cantillon and to a certain extent Baudeau) or planner of production (Say and to a certain extent Baudeau), and the English view, which saw in the entrepreneur chiefly a supplier and accumulator of capital. We have no reason to quarrel with this assessment, except that it may give the mistaken impression that the English theory of entrepreneurship was superior to the French.

JEAN-BAPTISTE SAY

The man of nineteenth-century economics whose name more than any other is identified with the entrepreneur is

J. B. Say (1767-1832), the first professor of economics in Europe. Say is regarded by contemporary economists as a disciple of Adam Smith, but this view does not do justice to Say's originality as a classical economist. Say's treatment of the nature and role of the entrepreneur, in particular, was far superior to Smith's.

By the time Say came to write abut the entrepreneur, the term had been used in various ways by Cantillon, Quesnay, Baudeau, Turgot, and others. But currency in the use of a term does not by itself establish intellectual lineage, and Say's theory of entrepreneurship had little in common with Cantillon's or the physiocrats'. While Cantillon's theory of entrepreneurship stressed the single function of bearing uncertainty, the physiocrats and Turgot emphasized various combinations of either the planning and organizing function, the innovating function, or the capital-supplying function. Say shared this multifaceted concept of the physiocrats, but on the whole he voiced opposition to their theories. Hoselitz (1960), who has done extensive research into the subject, maintains that Say's inspiration came primarily from his practical experience as an industrial entrepreneur (he ran a spinning factory in Pas-de-Calais) rather than his acquaintance with other French economists.

Say's discussion of entrepreneurship is most fully developed in the later editions of his *Traité d'économie politique* (1st edition, 1803) and in his *Cours complet d'économie politique pratique* (1st edition, 1828-29). It is a discussion that proceeds on two different levels. On the one hand, Say employed empirical descriptions of what entrepreneurs in his day actually did under certain institutional constraints. On the other hand, he exposed and analyzed the central function of the entrepreneur independently of any particular social framework. It is in this latter effort that he lays claim to a general theory of entrepreneurship. The difference in these two treatments of the subject is more a matter of scientific method than is first apparent, a point that has been effectively underscored in the following fashion by Hoselitz:

> The actual behavior patterns of entrepreneurs, their motives and objectives may display a considerable degree of variation, both

as between persons or industries, as well as between countries and geographical areas. The task of developing a theory of entrepreneurship consists in selecting those aspects of entrepreneurial behavior which are most significant and in determining the degree of generality with which they are found. In other words out of the manifold and different acts which entrepreneurs have performed or may be expected to perform one has to eliminate all those which are "accidental" or which are the result of special circumstances of the person, the time, the locality, the industry, or other factors. Those acts which are left constitute then the most typical forms of entrepreneurial behavior and we can then indicate how commonly they are found. This procedure results not only in an entrepreneurial theory, but indicates at the same time whether, and to what extent entrepreneurial activity is dependent upon certain institutional relations. (1960, p. 252)

One of the institutional relations upon which entrepreneurial activity clearly depends is the composition, distribution, and security of property rights. Because entrepreneurial activity is profit-seeking activity, it requires an incentive system to set it in motion. This incentive system is provided by the structure of private property rights within a representative government. Say was quite clear on this, avowing that "[p]olitical economy recognizes the right of property solely as the most powerful of all encouragements to the multiplication of wealth," and that where property exists in reality as well as right, "then, and then only, can the sources of production, namely, land, capital, and industry, attain their utmost degree of fecundity" (1845, p. 127).

Say's theory of the entrepreneur begins with his division of human industry into three distinct operations. The first step is the scientific one, whereby before any product, say, a bicycle, can be made, certain knowledge about the nature and purpose of it must be understood. It must be known, for example, that a wheel is capable of smooth, circular motion and that a force exerted on a chain and sprockets can propel the wheel forward. The second step — the "entrepreneurial" one — is the application of this knowledge to a useful purpose, that is, the development of a mechanism (the bicycle) with one or more wheels capable of transporting someone from one place to another.

The last step is the manufacturing of the item at the hands of manual labor.

In this schema, it should be obvious that the entrepreneur performs a social function, although Say does not make him a member of a distinct social class. He is a principal agent of production, as his role is vital to the production of useful goods. It should further be clear that the applications of knowledge made by the entrepreneur are not mere random events. Indeed, they must meet a "market test"; that is, each application must, in order to be "entrepreneurial," lead to the creation of value, or utility. This requires sound judgment, one of the key characteristics of Say's entrepreneur. This judgment is emphasized by Say in a number of ways. In his *Treatise* Say expounded it this way: To be an entrepreneur

> requires a combination of moral qualities, that are not often found together. Judgment, perseverance, and a knowledge of the world, as well as of business. He is called upon to estimate, with tolerable accuracy, the importance of the specific product, the probable amount of the demand, and the means of its production: at one time he must employ a great number of hands; at another, buy or order the raw material, collect labourers, find consumers, and give at all times a rigid attention to order and economy; in a word, he must possess the art of *superintendence* and *administration* [emphasis supplied]. (1845, pp. 330-31)

And how pivotal is the entrepreneur? In Say's view he is crucial because, although human industry requires all three operations mentioned above, it is the entrepreneur who is the catalyst. Say recognized that in carrying out his function the entrepreneur frequently puts himself at risk, but this is not the main strain of his argument, as it was for Cantillon. Again emphasizing judgment, Say affirmed that the entrepreneur

> is he who estimates needs and above all the means to satisfy them, who compares the end with these means. Hence his principal quality is to have good judgment. He can lack personal knowledge of science, by judiciously employing that of others, he can avoid dirtying his own hands by using the hands of others, but he must not lack judgment; for then he might produce at great expense something which has no value. (1840, vol. I, p. 100)

Risk is incidental to Say's notion of entrepreneurship because he saw no necessary relationship between entrepreneurial activity and capital accumulation. For the first time in economic literature, entrepreneurial activity became virtually synonymous with management, in the contemporary sense of that term. In this modern sense, management may, but does not necessarily, supply capital to the enterprise. Theoretically, at least, Say saw no difficulty in separating the entrepreneurial function from the capitalist function, even though both functions could be and often were combined in the same person. The basic distinction was that the entrepreneur-manager was an expert at superintendence and administration, whereas the capitalist was a lender of money. This distinction is not as sharp in Cantillon, although his meaning is quite clear that the entrepreneur is more than a mere capitalist.

Hoselitz (1960) has attempted to distinguish Say from Cantillon on two basic points, both of which appear to miss the mark. One point is that Say's entrepreneur is the universal mediator (between landlord and capitalist, between scientist and manual labor, between producers and consumers, and so on), and Cantillon's is not. Aside from the fact that Say's entrepreneurial theory (unlike Cantillon's) has no place for one of society's most active mediators, the arbitrageur, Hoselitz apparently did not read Cantillon's *Essai* closely. The entrepreneur is very much in evidence in that work as a central figure in the economy. His sole function is to mediate discrepancies between quantities demanded and supplied. Indeed, based on the somewhat superficial criterion of frequency of reference, the entrepreneur is much more prominent as mediator in Cantillon's work than he is in Say's writings.

Hoselitz's (1960) other point is that Say's entrepreneur — unlike Cantillon's and the physiocrats' — is not confined to a capitalist society. Although Hoselitz may be technically correct on this point, to argue in such a vein seems to go completely against the force of Say's argument, the chief aim of which was to reaffirm the desirable social consequences of individual self-interest. These consequences were attendant, in Say's view, on the kind of social framework that established and secured private property rights and encouraged capital accumulation.

However, Hoselitz is quite correct on another point: Say's entrepreneur (mediator) may appear even in a primitive society before capital has been accumulated. In other words, the entrepreneur could direct and superintend raw materials and manual labor without the application of capital. But surely this is true of Cantillon's beggar and robber entrepreneurs as well.

There is one final aspect of Say's entrepreneurship that is crucial for marking future departures in economic literature. Say's entrepreneur is, as it were, a "guardian" of equilibrium. The "judgment" extolled by Say as a requisite of entrepreneurial activity is confined to relations within a production process and does not extend beyond that process to the discovery of new processes or to changes inspired by a new social structure. Because he did not see a relationship between capital accumulation or investment and entrepreneurial activity, Say did not place the entrepreneur in a dynamic environment. His role was conceived within a purely stationary equilibrium characterized by the equality of prices of products with their costs of production. The primary source of entrepreneurial income under this system is not profit as a premium for risk but rather a wage as payment for a highly skilled type of scarce labor.

In the final analysis, Say (1845) presented the entrepreneur in economic theory as a kind of superior laborer. He extended this idea to the notion of a "market" for entrepreneurs in which their wages were determined by supply and demand considerations, and he went to some length to discuss the determinants of supply. From the standpoint of economic theory, his treatment of the entrepreneur was a step forward because it distinguished between the respective contributions in production of human and nonhuman agents. But in the broader context of the history of economic analysis, Say's theory was a retrenchment from the insights gained earlier by Cantillon and the physiocrats.* By representing the entrepreneur chiefly as a

---

*One French economist who took exception to Say's theory of entrepreneurship was Courcell-Seneuil (1813-1892), who insisted that profit is not a wage but is due to the assumption of risk. Knight (1921, p. 25n) attributes to him a glimpse of "the fact that the assumption of a 'risk' of error in one's judgment, inherent in the making of a responsible decision,

superior form of labor, Say consciously or unconsciously directed attention away from the uniqueness of the entrepreneurial role and from that agent's influence as a force of change in a dynamic economy.

---

is a phenomenon of a different character from the assumption of 'risk' in the insurance sense."

CHAPTER 5

DEAD ENDS, DETOURS,
AND REDIRECTIONS

Assuming the burden of the fluctuations in the expenditure
which must be made in any business and in the results attained
is . . . the distinctive mark of the entrepreneur.

H. von Mangoldt

ENGLISH CUSTOM BEFORE ADAM SMITH

There were three commonly used English equivalents
of the French term entrepreneur in the eighteenth century:
"adventurer," "projector," and "undertaker." The first term
was applied in the fifteenth century to merchants operating at
some risk, and in the seventeenth century to land speculators,
farmers, and those who directed certain public works projects.
During the eighteenth century, the term adventurer gradually
gave way to the more general term undertaker, which by the
time Smith wrote (in 1776), had become synonymous with an
ordinary businessman. The term projector was equivalent to
the other two in a fundamental sense, but it more often had the

pejorative connotation of a cheat and a rogue. The word under-taker was not only used more often but had more varied mean-ings, and its history more or less paralleled the development of its French counterpart.

At first, "undertaker" simply meant someone who set out to do a job or complete a project, but its meaning eventually funneled into the concept of government contractor — someone who, at his own financial risk, performed a task imposed on him by government. The term was later extended to include those individuals who held exclusive franchises from the Crown or the Parliament, for example, tax farmers, or those individuals commissioned to drain the fens. By and by the government connection was dropped, and the term simply came to designate someone involved in a risky project from which an uncertain profit might be derived (Hoselitz 1960, pp. 240-42). For reasons that are not clear, by the nineteenth century "under-taker" had acquired the special meaning of an arranger of funerals. Partly because of the example provided by Smith, the economic meaning of the term undertaker eventually came to be replaced by the term capitalist.

SMITH, RICARDO, AND THE "UNFORTUNATE LEGACY"

The *locus classicus* of economic analysis in the eighteenth century was Adam Smith's *Inquiry Into the Nature and Causes of the Wealth of Nations* (1776). Although a certified classic in the history of economics, it is notably deficient in one important sense. Smith failed to separate the entrepreneurial decision maker from among the various kinds of "industrious people" in the economy. He made passing references to both projectors and undertakers, but Smith infused neither of these terms with entrepreneurial content. The undertaker was regarded as a mere capitalist, and at that, he was, in Spengler's phrase, "a prudent, cautious, not overly imaginative fellow, who adjusts to circumstances rather than brings about their modifi-cation" (1959, pp. 8-9).

Smith observed that the profits of the undertaker constitute a reward for hazarding his stock (capital) in a particular venture.

Conforming to customary eighteenth-century usage, Smith linked the projector to speculative enterprises, noting that "establishment of any new manufacture, of any new branch of commerce, or of any new practice in agriculture, is always a speculation, from which the projector promises himself extraordinary profits" (1937, p. 114).

Indirect references to the entrepreneurial role are nevertheless present in Smith's magnum opus. For example, managerial decision making is clearly important in connection with the division of labor. Smith observed:

> The owner of the stock which employs a great number of labourers necessarily endeavors, for his own advantage, to make such a proper division and distribution of employment, that they may be enabled to produce the greatest quantity of work possible. (1937, p. 86)

Here again it is the capitalist that is singled out for attention. Further setting the pattern for the classical theory of income distribution, Smith denied the importance of "management" as a determinant of profit. On this last point, he was unequivocal, noting:

> The profits of stock, it may perhaps be thought, are only a different name for the wages of a particular sort of labour, the labour of inspection and direction. They are, however, altogether different, are regulated by quite sufficient principles, and bear no proportion to the quantity, the hardship, or the ingenuity of this supposed labour of inspection and direction. They are regulated altogether by the value of the stock employed, and are greater or smaller in proportion to the extent of this stock. (1937, p. 48)

The consequence of this declaration, and of Smith's overall neglect of the entrepreneurial function, is that classical economics failed to accord a separate share of output to the entrepreneur, thereby suggesting that any such return was not legitimate in a capitalist society. In the phrase of Redlich (1966, p. 715), this was a most unfortunate legacy. Through David Ricardo, this legacy was subsequently bequeathed to Karl Marx, who embellished and passed on the idea of the capitalist bogey, that is, the parasitic "extortionist" who sucks profit from the "industrious" people of the economy.

The paradox involved in Smith's treatment (or, more appropriately, nontreatment) of the entrepreneur is further heightened by the fact that he was very sensitive to the effects of innovation in a capitalist society. Indeed, Smith was one of the first economic writers to recognize innovation as a professional activity. In a remark on inventions made by workmen, Smith observed:

> Many improvements have been made by the ingenuity of the makers of the machines, when to make them became the business of a peculiar trade; and some by that of those who are called philosophers or men of speculation, whose trade it is not to do anything, but to observe everything; and who, upon that account, are often capable of combining together the powers of the most distant and dissimilar objects. (1937, p. 10)

It is difficult to see how the "philosophers" of this passage are any different from those we call innovative entrepreneurs (for example, a Thomas Edison), yet Smith did not develop this fruitful line of inquiry.

The eighteenth-century inventor (Smith's "philosopher" or "speculator") was an amateur by contemporary standards; yet Smith's view of innovation as professional activity was ahead of its time. He held that innovation is the product of the division of labor, which in turn depends on the extent of the market. Innovation therefore appears first in markets that are enlarged by cheap transportation. Opulence and progress thereafter accompany the division of labor, and with this progress the innovator or inventor becomes more specialized, and "the quantity of science is considerably increased."

Despite this noteworthy advance by the "father of economics," classical economics in general had very little to say about the origin and nature of investment opportunities. This is especially true of Ricardo (1772-1823), who assumed that capitalists act rationally in seeking to maximize profits but who shed no light on the nature of the trouble and risk involved in investing. Although he did not fall into the trap of assuming that all investment was profitable, like most classical economists Ricardo treated innovation as mainly external to the economic system. On occasion he supposed that as wealth increased, eventually all further opportunities for profitable investment would disappear. This stands in marked contrast to the Schumpeterian view, which was the first modern statement of innovation as professional activity within the economic system. Not only the scope but the breadth of entrepreneurial activity and investment opportunity were consequently enlarged in the Schumpeterian system.

In the context of our subject, there is a sense in which Ricardo is more culpable than Smith for his neglect of the entrepreneur. Smith was acquainted with Quesnay, and he may also have known Turgot's work directly. But aside from a difference in emphasis, Smith did not view the entrepreneur/undertaker in terms much different from his French counterparts' Ricardo, on the other hand, failed entirely to pursue Say's suggestion that the entrepreneur is distinguishable from the other agents of production. Smith could not have done so because his work preceded Say's, but Say had formalized the term entrepreneur and given it definition some 14 years before Ricardo's *Principles* appeared. Moreover, at least one version of Say's repeated notion was available to Ricardo in English during this 14-year period. Yet, as Cole noted, "not merely is the term [entrepreneur] itself absent in Ricardo's writings, but no concept of business leaders as agents of change (other than as shadowy bearers of technological improvements) is embraced in his treatment of economic principles" (1946, p. 3). It is noteworthy that in the correspondence between Say and Ricardo, neither the nature nor role of the entrepreneur is once mentioned, the usual discussion focusing instead on the topic of value.

JEREMY BENTHAM: THE ENTREPRENEUR AS CONTRACTOR

Ricardo played a major role in setting forth the "research program" that was to occupy the next generation of economists.

His failure to recognize the entrepreneur as a separate agent of production was therefore a harbinger of later developments in economic theory by writers in the Ricardian tradition. In the broader field of public policy, however, one British writer brought considerable attention to bear on the entrepreneur. That writer was Jeremy Bentham (1748-1832), whose ties with France and its intellectual tradition were much stronger than those of his contemporaries.

It is noteworthy that Bentham and Ricardo had different notions about what political economy should be. Ricardo saw political economy as a means to discover general laws of society. For him, economics was a theory detached from practice, whatever might subsequently be its practical consequences. To Ricardo, political economy was a science of laws — laws of equilibrium and laws of progress. By contrast, Bentham understood political economy in much the same way as his contemporary, Smith. He referred to economics as both art and science, and he paid as much attention to the former as he did to the latter. For Bentham, as for Smith, political economy was a branch of politics and legislation, never removed from practice. We cannot be sure whether it was Bentham's large concern for practice as well as theory that induced him to see the importance of the entrepreneur in economic activity. But it is a matter of record that he reproached Smith for his flogging efforts against projectors.

Like Smith, Bentham undersood that the regime most favorable to the development of inventive faculties was one of absolute liberalism. But, unlike Smith, Bentham (1952) defended usurers and projectors as useful sets of men. Both helped to advance the cause of inventive genius, each in his own way. It is something of a puzzle that Smith would, on the one hand, recognize innovation as a professional activity while on the other hand ignore its importance in another context. In his denunciation of usury, Smith failed to see the importance of the innovator. Bentham aptly pointed this out in his *Defence of Usury* (1787), the first publication that brought him public recognition as an economist. There Bentham detailed how laws against usury limit the overall quantity of capital lent and borrowed and how such laws keep away foreign money from domestic capital markets. Both these effects tend to throttle the activities of successful entrepreneurs. Although Bentham used the customary term projector, he was quite precise in his definition of this term as any person who, in the pursuit of wealth, strikes out into any new channel, especially into any channel of invention. Interest rate ceilings tend to discriminate against entrepreneurs of new projects, Bentham argued, because, by their novelty, such projects are more risky than those already proven profitable by experience. Moreover, legal restrictions of this sort are powerless to pick out bad projects from good ones.

In pleading the cause of the projectors, Bentham, the inventor of the Panopticon, was to some extent pleading his own case. Panopticon was the name Bentham gave to his idea of a model prison. The concept involved both an architectural and an institutional innovation. Bentham's ideal prison was designed to be circular with all the cells arranged concentrically round a central pavillion, which contained an inspector, or at most a small number of inspectors. From his central position the inspector could see at a glance everything that was going on, yet he was rendered invisible by a system of blinds. In this way, too, outside visitors could inspect the prisoners, as well as the prison's administration, without being seen. According to Bentham, this constant scrutiny of the prisoners would deprive them of the power, and even the will, to do evil. The site that Bentham proposed for his model prison is now occupied by the Tate Gallery in London. Bentham was never able to attract enough backers to make his model prison a reality.

The architectural idea behind the Panopticon was first applied in Russia by Bentham's brother Samuel, who in fact, deserves priority for the idea. Bentham's unique contribution was an administrative innovation that is more to the point of our subject than the general problem of prison reform. Bentham completed the architectural innovation of the Panopticon by introducing an administrative arrangement that involved management by contract. What is especially interesting about this arrangement is the critical way that its success depends on the dynamic activities of the entrepreneur and the proper structuring of economic incentives.

To Bentham, true reform would obtain in prisons only if the administrative plan simultaneously protected convicts against the harshness of their warders and society against the wastefulness of administrators. The choice, as he saw it, was between contract management and trust management. The differences are as follows:

> Contract-management is management by a man who treats with the government, and takes charge of the convicts at so much a head and applies their time and industry to his personal profit, as does a master with his apprentices. Trust-management is management by a single individual or by a committee, who keep up the establishment at the public expense, and pay into the treasury the products of the convicts' work. (Halévy 1955, p. 84)

In Bentham's mind, the latter arrangement did not provide the proper junction of interest and duty on the part of the entrepreneur. Its success therefore depends on "public interest" as a motivating factor. Bentham, like his proclaimed mentor, Smith, had much more confidence in individual self-interest as the spur to human action. The beauty of contract management was that it brought about an artificial identity of interests between the public on the one hand and the entrepreneur on the other. The entrepreneur in this case was an independent contractor who "purchased," through competitive bid, the right to run the prison, thereby also acquiring title to whatever profits might be earned by the application of convict labor. Such an entrepreneur-manager could maximize his long-term gains by preserving the health and productivity of his worker-convicts. In this manner public interest became entwined with private interest.

In 1787, Bentham completed the idea of contract management by a new administrative arrangement: He thought that life insurances offered an excellent means of joining the interest of one man to the preservation of a number of men. He therefore proposed that after consulting the appropriate mortality tables, the entrepreneur (prison manager) should be given a fixed sum of money for each convict due to die that year in prison, on condition that at the end of the year he must pay back the same sum for each convict who has actually died in prison. The difference would be profit for the entrepreneur, who would thereby have an economic incentive to lower the average mortality rate in his prison (Bentham 1962, vol. IV, p. 53).

Aside from the fact that Bentham was virtually alone among British classical economists in his repeated emphasis on the entrepreneur as an agent of economic progress, it is noteworthy that his administrative arrangement of contract management recast the entrepreneur in the position of government contractor, that is, a franchisee who undertakes financial risk in order to obtain an uncertain profit. Bentham also explicitly tied his notion of entrepreneur-contractor to the act of invention. He defended contract management as the proper form of prison administration on the ground that it is a progressive innovation and should therefore be rewarded accordingly, no less than an inventor is rewarded for his invention (1962, vol. IV, p. 47).

JOHN STUART MILL AND THE CLOSE OF THE CLASSICAL SYSTEM

We have seen that in British classical economics the entrepreneur was a persona non grata. If pressed, individual classical writers would probably have denied it, but the impression given by classical economics is that each business practically runs by itself. Certainly there had to be a merchant or undertaker who accumulated capital, but with this means he merely hires "industrious people" (workers) who do the rest. Such capital is exposed to risk of loss, but beyond this, all its owner does is to supervise his firm in order to guarantee that its profits find their way into his pocket. Say was the first to assign the entrepreneur a distinct position in the economic process apart from the capitalist, but even Say did not make full use of his important insight nor see clearly all of its analytic possibilities.

John Stuart Mill (1806-1873) was familiar with the works of Bentham and Say, yet he advanced the theory of entrepreneurship only a small step farther. Mill presented an analysis of business income that became the standard among economists for more than half a century. According to this theory, the businessman receives what Mill called the "wages of superintendence," which is a return for his special skill and ability as a manager. He further receives a premium for risk taking (although Mill did not progress as far as Cantillon in elaborating this point). Finally, the businessman receives interest on the owned part of the capital he employs. There is nothing in this last item to suggest any difference between the entrepreneur and the capitalist, although there may be something in the other two. Mill, however, failed to carry the analysis forward, so that in the end, all we can say is that he wished to make risk bearing an entrepreneurial function along with "direction." Also, it was Mill who brought the term entrepreneur into general use among English economists. On the entrepreneur as innovator, Mill had nothing important to say.

GERMAN PERFORMANCES IN THE CLASSICAL PERIOD

In Germany the analysis of the entrepreneurial function developed slowly but steadily within a tradition of economic science that emphasized administration and policy. This analysis took a major step forward in the work of J. H. von Thünen (1783-1850) and culminated in the later work of H. K. von Mangoldt (1824-1868).

Thünen is best known in the history of economics for his contributions to location theory, but in the second volume of *The Isolated State* (1850) he set forth an explanation of profit that clearly distinguished the return of the entrepreneur from that of the capitalist. What Thünen labeled "entrepreneurial gain" is profit minus (1) interest on invested capital, (2) insurance against business losses, and (3) the wages of management. This residual represents, for Thünen, a return to entrepreneurial risk. This last item Thünen identified as uninsurable risk, insofar as "there exists no insurance company that will cover all and every risk connected with a business. A part of the risk must always be accepted by the entrepreneur" (1960, p. 246).

As Kanbur (1980) has argued, opportunity costs provide the basis for measuring this element of risk. Thünen seems to have had the same argument in mind when he wrote:

> He who has enough means to pay to get some knowledge and education for public service has a choice to become either a civil servant or, if equally suited for both kinds of jobs, to become an industrial entrepreneur. If he takes the first job, he is guaranteed subsistence for life; if he chooses the latter, an unfortunate economic situation may take all his property, and then his fate becomes that of a worker for daily wages. Under such unequal expectations for the future what could motivate him to become an entrepreneur if the probability of gain were not much greater than that of loss? (1960, p. 247)

Thünen clearly appreciated the difference between management and entrepreneurship. He maintained that the effort of an entrepreneur working on his own account was different from that of a paid substitute ("manager"), even if they have the same knowledge and ability. The entrepreneur is open to the anxiety and agitation that accompanies his business gamble; he spends many sleepless nights preoccupied with the single thought of how to avoid catastrophe, whereas the paid substitute, if he has worked well during the day and finds himself tired in the evening, can sleep soundly, secure in the knowledge of having performed his duty. Anyone who has nursed along a new enterprise knows precisely of what Thünen speaks.

What is especially interesting about Thünen's treatment is how he turns the discussion from the trials of the entrepreneur into a kind of "crucible" theory of the development of entrepreneurial talent. The sleepless nights of the entrepreneur are not unproductive; it is then that the entrepreneur makes his plans and arrives at solutions for avoiding business failure. Adversity in the business world thereby becomes a training ground for the entrepreneur. As Thünen put it:

> Necessity is the mother of invention; and so the entrepreneur through his troubles will become an inventor and explorer in his field. So, as the invention of a new and useful machine rightly gets the surplus which its application provides in comparison with an older machine, and this surplus is the compensation for his invention, in the same way what the entrepreneur brings about by greater mental effort in comparison with the paid manager is compensation for his industry, diligence, and ingenuity. (1960, p. 248)

What makes this a significant step forward in the theory of entrepreneurship is the fact that Thünen successfully married the separate strands of entrepreneurial theory that, on the one hand, characterized the entrepreneur as risk bearer (Cantillon, Mill), and, on the other hand, portrayed him as innovator (Baudeau, Bentham). Economic analysis having come this far by 1850, we may well question whether Joseph Schumpeter took a step backward in the next century by excluding risk bearing from the nature of entrepreneurship, confining its meaning instead solely to innovative activity (see Chapter 7).

Thünen was quite explicit about the fact that there are two elements in entrepreneurial income: a return to "entrepreneurial risk" and a return to ingenuity. Labeling the sum of these two as "business profit," Thünen drew a succinct and precise distinction between entrepreneurship and capital use:

> Capital will give results, and is in the strict sense of the term capital, only if used productively; on the degree of this usefulness depends the rate of interest at which we lend capital. Productive use presupposes an industrial enterprise and an entrepreneur. The enterprise gives the entrepreneur a net yield after compensating for all expanses and costs. This net yield has two parts, business profits and capital use. (1960, p. 249)

A clearer distinction between these two essential factors of production was difficult to find in the economic literature that preceded Thünen.

As pertains to our subject, the other leading light in Germany during this period was Hans Karl Emil von Mangoldt, professor at the universities of Göttingen and Frieburg. Mangoldt's works remain inaccessible to those not at home in the German language, but we know of the significance of his contribution through the notice taken of him by Knight (1921), Schumpeter (1954), Hutchison (1953), and Hennings (1980). Knight attributed to Mangoldt "a most careful and exhaustive analysis of profit" (1921, p. 27), and Schumpeter assessed his work on entrepreneurship as "the most important advance since Say" (1954, p. 556n).

Mangoldt undertook a reform of the entrepreneurial theory of F. B. W. von Hermann (1795-1868), a politician, civil servant, and teacher who strode beyond Ricardo in the fundamentals of economic theory, particularly in his supply and demand approach to the theory of value. Hermann turned to the personal activity of entrepreneurs in respect to their businesses in order to find the essential characteristic that makes them entrepreneurs. He held that certain kinds of labor are inseparable from the concept of the entrepreneur and that these tasks could not be delegated to anyone else without the delegating party ceasing to be an entrepreneur. Among these tasks Hermann reckoned the assembling of capital, the supervision of business, the securing of credit and trade connections, and the assumption of risk associated with the prospect of irregular gains. Mangoldt discarded the first three as inessential to the concept of the entrepreneur. Although as a rule entrepreneurs participate in their own enterprises with their own capital and personal supervision, Mangoldt argued that these services could just as well be furnished by salaried labor and are not therefore part of entrepreneurial activity. What remains is risk bearing. According to Mangoldt, "That which alone is inseparable from the concept of the entrepreneur is, on the one hand, owning the output of the undertaking – control over the product brought forth, and, on the other hand, assuming responsibility for whatever losses may occur" (1907, p. 41).

Mangoldt's theory of entrepreneurship was production-oriented and risk-centered. He distinguished between "production to order" and "production for the market." The former is safe because service and payment are simultaneous, thereby eliminating the uncertainty of changing market conditions between the start of production and sale of the final product. The latter is speculative because the product is destined for exchange on a market of uncertain demand and unknown price. Mangoldt found this distinction useful, even though it is imprecise.

> Strictly interpreted, every possibility of a change in the subjective estimate of the service, or the remuneration, offers such an uncertainty; and, on that account, since such a possibility is excluded only by a perfect simultaneity of service and payment, every business which needs for its carrying through any time

whatever, could not, in the strictest sense of the word, be undertaken to order. (1907, p. 37)

The significance of the distinction is that it provides a means of discussing degrees of risk that might befall the entrepreneur. Those enterprises that require the longest time to bring their products to the point of final sale involve the most uncertainty by Mangoldt's reckoning, whereas those that involve the shortest time require the least amount of entrepreneurship. Risk goes to the heart of the matter. The distinctive mark of Mangoldt's entrepreneur is that he assumes the burden of the fluctuations in expenditure that must be made in any business and in the consequent outcome of the enterprise. In this respect he stood squarely in the Cantillon tradition.

Mangoldt also developed the notion that entrepreneurial profit is the rent of ability, and he insisted that the entrepreneur be treated as a separate factor of production. He divided entrepreneurial income into three parts: a premium on uninsurable risks; entrepreneur interest and wages, including only payments for special forms of capital or productive effort that did not admit of exploitation by anyone other than the owner; and entrepreneur rents, that is, payments for differential abilities or assets not held by anyone else. Alfred Marshall (1961, vol. II, p. 462) took special note of this last item, citing Mangoldt approvingly in his development of the principle of quasi-rent.

Mangoldt's theory did not concentrate on an ideal type of entrepreneur but rather on the decisions he must make in an uncertain, competitive environment: the choice of techniques, the allocation of productive factors, and the marketing of production. Although he recognized that successful innovation is part of entrepreneurship, Mangoldt nevertheless expressed more interest in the allocative function of the entrepreneur. His contribution therefore belongs more to the static theory of resource allocation than to the dynamic theory of growth and development.

Both Thünen and Mangoldt were important anticipators of Knight (see Chapter 6), who in the next century revived Cantillon's idea of the entrepreneur as risk bearer. Thünen's contribution may be judged the more significant of the two, however, insofar as it combined elements of risk bearing and innovation in a way that pointed past the concept of entrepreneurship that has until recently dominated twentieth-century literature on the subject.

CHAPTER 6

THE ENTREPRENEUR
RESURRECTED

The central figure in the productive system is the entrepreneur.

F. Y. Edgeworth

The entrepreneur is any legal owner of an enterprise.

F. von Wieser

THE NEOCLASSICAL VIEW

The neoclassical period of economic analysis marked a turning away from the macro concerns of economic growth and income distribution as primary points of attention by economic writers toward a fundamental concern with the microeconomic foundations of price formation. This redirection was ushered in by a radical new emphasis on the role of demand considerations, as seen through marginal utility evaluations of individuals, over cost considerations in the calculation of economic value. But for a few notable exceptions, economic analysis after 1870

51

became increasingly abstract and mechanistic, the economic problem coming to be conceived as the allocation of certain scarce means among given ends rather than the selection of the ends themselves. In this era, no longer did the great macro concerns of the classical period (for example, population, capital supply, economic growth) dominate economic inquiry. The new economic analysis was developed by a novel breed of professional economists who, unlike their predecessors of the previous period, received university training and took up teaching positions in the new discipline. Consequently they were less firmly rooted in the parent discipline of philosophy and simultaneously more open to the applications of mathematics to economic reasoning. All of this underlay the subtle change of terminology that saw "economics" undermine and eventually replace the older term political economy.

We have seen how the English variant of the old paradigm (Smith-Ricardo-Mill) tended to conflate the roles of capitalist and entrepreneur. For its part, neoclassical value theory did not develop a theory of enterprise, and only grudgingly did it yield a theory of capital. Consequently, marginal utility theory did not limit the range of possible differences of opinion concerning the entrepreneur. The new paradigm took ends as given, explained allocation of scarce resources to meet these given ends, and focused attention on equilibrium results rather than adjustment processes. It therefore left no room for entrepreneurial action; the entrepreneur became a mere automaton, a passive onlooker with no real scope for individual decision making. Certain writers in the neoclassical tradition nevertheless kept alive the critical importance of the entrepreneur; some even advanced the theory. This chapter attempts to survey developments in the latter regard.

MARSHALL AND HIS CIRCLE

Alfred Marshall's (1842-1924) accomplishments as a synthesizer of classical thought are prodigious; however, his intellectual contributions toward the topic of entrepreneurship do not match his legacy in other areas. Aware of the writings of

Cantillon and Say on the role of the entrepreneur as an important element within a well-conceived theory of economic progress, Marshall nevertheless opted for the more traditional English scenario of the entrepreneur (or more precisely the undertaker) as a multifaceted capitalist.

In this regard Marshall may have been heavily influenced by Ricardo and Mill. He made no explicit functionary statements, so his ideas about the role of the entrepreneur can only be inferred from his writings about the "earnings of management." Marshall's chief statements in this regard were in the area of income distribution. From his discussions of this topic, some insights can be gleaned about why the entrepreneur was remunerated.

This inferential approach is spawned by Marshall's tendency to treat Mill's undertaker as a person analogous to Say's entrepreneur. Mill's "wages of superintendence" referred to payments for more than mere business management (see Chapter 5). But it was Marshall, in his *Principles of Economics* (1890), who gave us some insight into what were the responsibilities of superintendence. There he informed us that a superintendent is both "a merchant and organizer of production" (1961, p. 297). It is not clear whether the superintendent is also a capitalist. As a merchant and organizer he must forecast "the broad movements of production and consumption" and discern "where there is an opportunity for supplying a new commodity that will meet a real want or improv[e] the plan of producing an old commodity" (1961, p. 297). In order to accomplish this task, the superintendent "must be able to judge cautiously and undertake risks boldly" (1961, p. 297).

In these selected passages are the ingredients for Marshall to have extended Cantillon's idea of the entrepreneur as an uncertainty bearer. We can only speculate as to why he did not; perhaps the entrepreneur-capitalist tie of his classical forebears was too strong for him to break through the old mold.

Marshall added the element of leadership to Mill's list of "entrepreneurial" responsibilities. Marshall's businessman "must be a natural leader of men" who can choose assistants wisely but also exercise "a general control over everything" and preserve "order and unity in the main plan of business" (1961,

p. 298). In fulfilling this organizational function, the entrepreneur must always be "on the lookout for . . . methods that promise to be more effective in proportion to their cost than methods currently in use" (1961, p. 359).*

Marshall was keenly aware that not everyone had the innate ability to perform this entrepreneurial role: These "abilities are so great and so numerous that very few persons can exhibit them all in a very high degree" (1961, p. 298). There is, however, a remuneration for successfully exercising these entrepreneurial talents, and it was one of Marshall's special insights that enabled him to break away from the stultifying wages-fund doctrine and associate the "earnings of management" with the notion of a surplus, or more specifically, a "quasi-rent." This "quasi-rent," according to Marshall, is a return for

> exceptional natural abilities, which are not made by human effort, and are not the result of sacrifices undergone for a future gain, they enable him [the entrepreneur] to obtain a surplus income over what ordinary persons could expect for similar exertions following similar investments of capital and labour in their education and start in life.† (1961, p. 623)

Although Marshall carried forward the Mill-Mangoldt notion of rent-of-ability, it is noteworthy that his treatment of the entrepreneur omits any serious discussion of invention and innovation. He was writing at the high tide of competitive capitalism in England and on the Continent. Observably, economic growth had resulted from productive initiatives in industry. Yet, although Marshall was undoubtedly aware of the importance of innovation in society, he made no explicit

---

*Harbison (1956, p. 356) asserts that Marshall's concept of the functions of the entrepreneur applies not to a single individual but rather to a hierarchy of individuals. Accordingly, the Marshallian entrepreneur is in essence "*an organization* which comprises all of the people required to perform entrepreneurial functions."

†This idea, Schumpeter (1954) conjectured, is an outgrowth of Mangoldt's theory of rent of ability and supranormal returns to personal exertion. Indeed, Marshall cited Mangoldt approvingly in this connection.

connections between successful entrepreneurial activities and innovation or between innovation and economic growth (Shove 1942).

Francis Y. Edgeworth (1845-1926), who considered himself a disciple of Marshall's, reflected the Marshallian concept of the entrepreneur. Edgeworth may have been the first English writer to use the word entrepreneur, but he commandeered only the term, not its distinctive French meaning. For Edgeworth the sphere of influence of the entrepreneur was entirely within the firm; the results of entrepreneurial actions did not impact on economic growth.

> The central figure in the productive system is the entrepreneur. [He] buy[s] the factors of production, the use of land, labour, machinery, and work[s] them up into half-manufactured or finished products, which he sells to other entrepreneurs or consumers, at a price covering his expenses and remunerating his work and waiting.* (1925, p. 378)

As might be expected, Edgeworth failed to move the concept of the entrepreneur outside the Marshallian paradigm. Even if he were "the echo of Marshall's voice," as Schumpeter (1954, pp. 920-21) claims, Edgeworth was, nevertheless, a man of considerable talents and insights. He knew Mill's work, as might be expected of a Marshallian, but he was also aware of contributions by Francis A. Walker and F. B. Hawley (discussed below), which suggests that he was familiar with the risk-related dimensions of entrepreneurship inter alia. He failed, however, to develop anything like a full-blown theory of entrepreneurship.

One of Marshall's students, A. C. Pigou (1877-1959), shunted the theory of entrepreneurship onto an even more narrow track, returning to the traditional Smithian view of the entrepreneur as a capitalist. After 1850, methods of business financing had changed so that the entrepreneur-capitalist association was less common (Zrinyi 1962). Nevertheless, Pigou associated entrepreneurs with financiers, who, as stockholders,

---

*This statement compares favorably with Cantillon's vision (see Chapter 3) except for one critical difference. Edgeworth seems to view entrepreneurial activity as being free from risk or uncertainty.

owned the production process: "The entrepreneurs . . . by whom the stream of goods that comes to completion every year is legally owned, sell these goods for money to wholesale houses and shopkeepers" (1929, p. 132).

In one significant sense, though, Pigou departed from the Marshall-Edgeworth tradition by acknowledging the societal impact of entrepreneurial activities. He held that the activities of entrepreneurs affected industrial fluctuations because they operated in an environment characterized by uncertainty. Pigou observed that

> [b]usiness men in making [production] forecasts are shadowed by immense uncertainties. . . . The immediate cause lying behind general movements of employment consists in shifts in the expectation of business men about future prospects, or, if we prefer a looser term, business confidence. (1949, p. 216)

Over the next 30 years or so, British thinking on this subject did not change much, as evidenced by the lack of a more complete concept of the entrepreneur in the theory of John Maynard Keynes (1883-1946), who was also one of Marshall's students. Keynes has been a wellspring of modern ideas in economics, most of which, however, have little to do with entrepreneurship. He treated the entrepreneur rather perfunctorily, retaining some conceptual notions of the entrepreneur as financier — the residual claimant of profit. Like Marshall, Keynes placed the entrepreneur in the role of decision maker within the individual firm. His function is to "fix the amount of employment at that level which [is] expect[ed] to maximize the excess of the proceeds over the factor costs" (Keynes 1964, p. 25). Put another way, Keynes's entrepreneur is an equity owner who is chiefly responsible for making investment decisions. As an active factor of production, he must face uncertainty in his ability to forecast "effective demand." The significance of uncertainty in the Keynesian paradigm has generally been understated by all but a few of Keynes's disciples, yet in many respects it was his most revolutionary contribution. The well-worn story in the history of economic thought is that Keynes's concern with macroeconomic variables subsequently served to shift economists' attention away from the entrepreneur toward the performance of certain aggregates in the economy. However true this may be, there is another side to *The General Theory*. Keynes's focus on uncertainty in decision making, and more generally on expectations, provides a link between the Marshallian "entrepreneur as manager" notion and the contemporary theory of enterprise and radical uncertainty put forward by Keynes's disciple G. L. S. Shackle (see Chapter 8).

Be that as it may, Keynes's discussion of the animus behind entrepreneurial activity is distinctly uneconomic and must be approached with caution. His comment on the nature of entrepreneurial uncertainty is that "business men play a mixed game of skill and chance, the average results of which to the players are not known by those who take a hand" (1964, p. 150). This statement is innocuous enough, but then Keynes does something extraordinary. He links enterprise not to calculations of expected profit but to "animal spirits" — the spontaneous urge to action declared to be innate in the human psyche. According to Keynes

> It is safe to say that enterprise which depends on hopes stretching into the future benefits the community as a whole. But individual initiative will only be adequate when reasonable calculation is supplemented and supported by animal spirits, so that the thought of ultimate loss which overtakes pioneers, as experience undoubtedly tells us and them, is put aside as a healthy man puts aside the expectation of death. (1964, p. 161)

In the final analysis, Keynes's explanation of entrepreneurial activity rests as much on whim, sentiment, or chance as it does on rational expectations of profit opportunities. As such, it is an analytical dead end, deserving little further comment or attention.

THE AUSTRIAN SCHOOL

With the publication of his pioneering *Principles of Economics* (1871), Carl Menger (1840-1921) established himself as the founder and early leader of a distinctively Austrian school that later included two able disciples, Friedrich von Wieser and Eugen von Böhm-Bawerk. The central concern of Menger's economics was to establish the subjectivist perspective of human valuation as the starting point of economic theory. In the subjectivist view, economic change arises from an individual's awareness and understanding of circumstances rather than from the circumstances, per se. Thus Menger's analysis, as both Erich Streissler (1972) and Israel Kirzner (1979a) have pointed out, relied heavily on the role of knowledge in individual decisions.

In later chapters we shall see how Menger's vision served as a basis for more recent theories of entrepreneurship developed by various writers inside and outside the Austrian tradition. That vision was original and far-flung, even though the entrepreneur does not stand out as a prominent thread woven throughout his economic theory. Menger's entrepreneur is constantly in the background orchestrating production, and it is to the theory of production that one must look for an appreciation of the entrepreneurial role.

Menger's theory of production starts with the general theory of the good. For something to be a good in the economic sense requires recognition of the causal connection between useful things and the satisfaction of human needs, as well as action taken to direct the useful things to this satisfaction. In other words, the goods character of any useful thing is not innate; it must be acquired through human action, that is, recognition of a need, capability of satisfying that need, and action taken to do so. In the Austrian framework, goods can be ranked according to their causal connections. To use Menger's (1950, p. 56) example, the bread we eat, the flour from which it is baked, the grain milled into flour, and the field on which the grain is grown are all goods. But some goods serve individual needs directly, and some stand in a more remote causal connection. The former are called goods of "lower order"; the latter, goods of "higher order." The farther removed a good is from satisfying a want directly, the higher the number assigned to it in Menger's scale of goods-ordering. Thus bread is a good of first order because it satisfies hunger directly. Flour is a second-order good because it is one step removed from the direct satisfaction of need. The grain from which flour is milled, along with the mill and labor expended on it, are third-order goods. The field, farmers, and equipment used to grow grain are fourth-order goods, and so on.

From the foregoing we can see that to designate the order of a particular good is to indicate that in some particular employment it has a closer or more distant causal relationship with the satisfaction of a human need. For Menger, the ultimate goods character of higher order goods depends on the power to transform goods of higher order into goods of lower order. Economic production is the process by which this transformation takes place and by which the goods of lower order are directed finally into the satisfaction of human needs. This process is inseparable from the idea of time. Over time improvements in technology and transportation tend continually to shorten the time between phases of transforming higher order goods into lower order goods, but the time gaps never disappear completely. It is impossible to transform higher order goods into lower order goods by a mere wave of the hand. Production is never instantaneous.

Menger's conception of the entrepreneur, although never elaborated in any great detail, fits into the vision of production just outlined. This general theory of production leads to a conceptualization of the entrepreneur as one who must deal with the intertemporal coordination of the factors of production (that is, higher order goods). Menger recognized that industry is vertically disintegrated and that somebody has to align productive resources over time. That somebody is the entrepreneur. Ironically, the entrepreneur's own technical labor services are usually among the higher order goods he has at his command for purposes of production. Nevertheless, it is not the supply of such services that makes one an entrepreneur; it is instead his calculating and decision-making abilities that make his function unique. According to Menger:

Entrepreneurial activity includes: (a) obtaining *information* about the economic situation; (b) economic *calculation* — all the various computations that must be made if a production process is to be efficient; (c) the *act of will* by which goods of higher order are assigned to a particular production process; and finally (d) *supervision* of the execution of the production plan so that it may be carried through as economically as possible. (1950, p. 160)

An obvious corollary of Menger's conception of entrepreneurial activity is that the entrepreneur must face uncertainty with regard to the quantity and quality of final goods he can produce with the goods of higher order in his possession. The degree of uncertainty faced by the entrepreneur depends on the extent of his knowledge of the productive process and upon the degree of control he exercises over it. Menger recognized this fact and underscored its importance:

> Human uncertainty about the quantity and quality of the product of the whole causal process is greater the larger the number of elements involved in any way in the production of consumption goods which we either do not understand or over which, even understanding them, we have no control. . . . This uncertainty . . . is of the greatest practical significance in human economy. (1950, p. 71)

Menger did not attempt to link the entrepreneur with the capitalist, and, indeed, it would have been a step backward for entrepreneurial theory had he done so. But his position with regard to risk bearing is curious, especially in the face of repeated emphasis on the significance of uncertainty in economic affairs. Despite the fact that the entrepreneur must continually contend with uncertainty in the process of production, Menger held that risk bearing cannot be the essential function of the entrepreneur. Noting his departure from Mangoldt on this issue, Menger (1950, p. 161) asserted that risk is insignificant to entrepreneurship because in the final analysis the chance of loss is offset by the chance of gain.*

---

*The meaning of this statement, and its implications, are not quite clear. A counterbalancing tendency between gains and losses might be posited in a long-run analysis where all "projects" are lumped together (cf. Wieser 1927, p. 355). But from an individualist perspective, this assertion

It is interesting to speculate whether Menger's treatment of risk vis-a-vis entrepreneurship influenced a later "Austrian," Joseph Schumpeter (see Chapter 7), who also denied risk bearing as an essential characteristic of entrepreneurship. The outcome of such speculation remains problematic, but Schumpeter's vision went beyond Menger's in the sense that his entrepreneur was a driving force in the process of economic development. In fact, Schumpeter virtually stood Menger on his head. Whereas Menger (1950) saw economic progress as leading to the development of entrepreneurial activity, Schumpeter viewed entrepreneurial activity as leading to economic progress.

Wieser (1851-1926), a student of Karl Knies's but a follower of Menger's, extended the latter's ideas and added several important dimensions to his entrepreneur, among them leadership, alertness, and risk bearing. Wieser defined the entrepreneur in a "legalistic" but otherwise catholic fashion:

> [T]he entrepreneur . . . is the director by legal right and at the same time by virtue of his active participation in the economic management of his enterprise. He is a leader in his own right. He is the legal representative of the operation, the owner of the material productive goods, creditor for all accounts receivable and debtor for all accounts payable. As a lessor or lessee he is obligated or privileged. He is the employer under all contracts for work and labor. . . . His economic leadership commences with the establishment of the enterprise; he supplies not only the necessary capital but originates the idea, elaborates and puts into operation the plan, and engages collaborators. When the enterprise is established, he becomes its manager technically as well as commercially. (1927, p. 324)

As is apparent from this passage, Wieser tried to bring everything connected with the theory and practice of enterprise under his umbrellalike definition of the entrepreneur. He spoke of entrepreneurs as the "great personalities" of capitalism: "bold

---

seems tantamount to the statement that each entrepreneurial opportunity has a 50-50 chance of success. Surely there is no a priori nor observed reason why this should be the case. In fact, Hawley and Clark later refuted this position (see below).

technical innovators, organizers with a keen knowledge of human nature, farsighted bankers, reckless speculators, the world-conquering directors of the trusts" (1927, p. 327).

This is painting with a broad brush. Not only is Wieser's multifarious entrepreneur a director, leader, employer, owner, capitalist, and innovator, "he must [also] possess the quick perception that seizes new terms in current transactions as his affairs develop; [and] he must possess the independent force-fulness to regulate his business according to his views." Finally, he must have the courage to accept risk and be driven forward by "the joyful power to create" (1927, p. 324).

Wieser's discussion touched themes that would be expounded again in the next two generations of entrepreneurial theories. Schumpeter (see Chapter 7) zeroed in on the innovating spirit and the creativity of entrepreneurs. Kirzner (see Chapter 8) elaborated the perceptiveness theme. As a rule, modern theories of entrepreneurship have averted the multifarious personality of the entrepreneur in favor of a more narrowly defined figure. Wieser, too, eventually admitted that institutional changes, primarily in forms of business organization, had gradually transformed the notion of entrepreneur to a mere legal concept. In the wake of such changes Wieser declared: "The requirement of economic management is no longer fulfilled in all cases. Today the enterprise is a voluntary community of commercial operation in the money economy subject to one entrepreneur. It may be a unified group of such operations. The entrepreneur is any legal owner of an enterprise" (1927, p. 328).

The third member of the Austrian triumvirate, Böhm-Bawerk (1851-1914), wrote very little about the entrepreneur, concerning himself primarily wth the theory of capital and interest. Schumpeter (1954, p. 893) has alluded to Böhm-Bawerk's uncertainty theory of profits, in which the source of entrepreneurs' profits is that things do not work out as planned. According to the theory, persistence of positive profits in a firm is a consequence of superior judgment in the face of uncertainty. We also have it on Murray Rothbard's (1980) authority that Böhm-Bawerk clearly identified the entrepreneur with the capitalist and that he in no way suggested that they could be separated. Be that as it may, Böhm-Bawerk did not develop his theory of profit and loss to any great extent, leaving this task to be accomplished by his student Mises (Chapter 8) and by the American economist Knight.

WALRAS'S NEGATIVE CONTRIBUTION

One of the most panoramic and unique visions of economic theory was exercised by the French economist Leon Walras (1834-1910), who elaborated the all-pervasive interdependence of economic affairs. The theory of general static equilibrium that he developed shows us a state of ultimate and timeless adjustment maintained by the competitive self-interest of the individual suppliers of productive services. In this world each productive service contributes technically and essentially to the production, transport, and sale of goods, thereby earning each day that amount by which the withdrawal of one such productive unit would reduce the daily output of the system as a whole. Furthermore, in this analytic system the total of all the payments to the suppliers of productive services exactly exhausts their total product.

To explore the full range of implications for economics emanating from this Walrasian vision would take us far afield of our subject. As regards that subject, however, we must agree with Schumpeter (1954, p. 893), a great admirer of Walras, that the latter's contribution was essentially negative. He introduced into his system the figure of the entrepreneur who neither gains nor loses, implying that in perfect competition, firms (that is, entrepreneurs) would break even in an equilibrium state. Even more crucial is the fact that Walras excluded time in all its interesting and significant aspects from his model. The result was a model that worked like a predictable, impersonal, and frictionless machine. In Shackle's phrase, it was an "inhuman model" (1955, p. 91). The real world consists of men's power and ambition to alter their economic environment over time, not merely respond to it. Walras's predictable, formalistic system was undoubtedly helpful, analytically, in stimulating clear thinking on many important economic phenomena, but on their own, purely mechanistic models cannot convey the full range of economic activity. For this reason, contemporary theories of entrepreneurship, Schumpeter's excepted, seem to have a pronounced anti-Walrasian bias.

AMERICAN INSIGHTS

Although American economics did not fully come into its own until the twentieth century, several key writers recognized the significance of the entrepreneur earlier than that. Chief among them were Francis Walker (1840-1897), who served as first president of the American Economic Association, Frederick Hawley (1843-1929), and the preeminent American economist of the period, John Bates Clark (1847-1938).

Walker's *Political Economy* (1884) preceded Marshall's *Principles* by six years and anticipated Marshall on several points, one being the treatment of profits as a form of rent. Like Keynes, Walker viewed the entrepreneur as an employer of workers. He variously described the entrepreneur as decision maker and leader, a "captain of industry," a "master," and a "higher" type of labor. Following the French economists, Walker separated the ownership of capital from the responsibilities of the entrepreneur.* His clearest description of the entrepreneurial function is in *The Wages Question*:

> [The entrepreneur's role is] to furnish technical skills, commercial knowledge, and powers of administration; to assume responsibilities and provide against contingencies; to shape and direct production, and to organize and control the industrial machine. (1876, p. 245)

Another American economist who insisted on the functional separation of entrepreneur and capitalist was Hawley. Hawley was a keen student of classical economics, but he was

---

*Thomas Cochran (1968) contends that the early development of modern corporations in the United States may have helped American writers perceive entrepreneurship as a function quite apart from that of the owner of capital.

also a fiercely independent thinker who made up his own mind on analytic issues. He seems to have been led to a study of entrepreneurship by his desire to refute a contestable issue in Böhm-Bawerk's theory of capital and interest. Hawley asserted that it is impossible to understand why capital has a price unless "we study industrial phenomena from the undertaker's point of view" (1892, p. 281). In a series of turn-of-the-century articles in the *Quarterly Journal of Economics*, Hawley developed a risk theory of profit that he set against the Böhm-Bawerkian view. His theory emphasized the entrepreneur as the great dynamic force of a capitalist economy. He ranked enterprise, or "risk taking," with land, labor, and capital as the four basic forces of production, and he characterized profit as the income arising from the chance of gain being greater than the loss in the risks assumed by the entrepreneur.

To Hawley risk and uncertainty were even more pervasive than capital in the industrial system. He contended that

> [t]here is . . . in all industrial undertakings in which capital is engaged, and in some also in which capital is not engaged, an element of risk which the final consumer has to pay for. And the reason is this: that everybody except the gambler — everybody, that is, engaged in industry — prefers a certainty to an uncertainty. (1892, p. 285)

Although apparently unknown to him, Hawley's formulation of risk was precisely the same as Cantillon's. The special peculiarity of every business risk, he asserted, "is surely no other than the uncertainty of how the selling price of an unsold product will compare with the cost, or how the cost of an unfinished product will compare with the selling price, if the latter has been agreed upon"* (Hawley, 1893, p. 464). There is also a slight Benthamite strain in Hawley's argument insofar as he recognized that some elements of costs could be fixed through insurance. But it was Clark who made Hawley aware of the distinction between insurable and noninsurable risk.

---

*Compare with Cantillon's vision, as portrayed by Hoselitz (1960, p. 240), that the entrepreneur is someone who buys at a certain cost price and sells at an uncertain price.

Hawley's ideas on entrepreneurship were provocative enough to spark a lively debate between him and Clark, who, at the turn of the century, was the leading figure of American economics. Clark acknowledged that Hawley and Mangoldt (whose work was unknown to Hawley) had successfully overturned a misconception of the Austrian theorists by pointing out that "men do not hazard their capital for an amount of annual gains that in a long term of years will just offset their losses. They demand more than this and they get it" (1892, p. 40). However, Clark refused to concede that risk bearing was an entrepreneurial activity. He argued, as Schumpeter also did at a later date, that all risk is borne by the capitalist. Clark used the term entrepreneur "in an unusually strict sense, to designate the man who coordinates capital and labor without in his own proper capacity furnishing either of them" (1892, pp. 45-46). It was his view that "the entrepreneur, as such, is empty-handed," a phrase evocative of Kirzner's "pure and penniless" entrepreneur (see Chapter 8). In other words, the entrepreneur cannot risk anything because he has nothing to risk.

In later works, Clark couched his discussion in terms of statics and dynamics, giving a role to the entrepreneur that inspired Schumpeter to an eventual new formulation. The static state in Clark's analysis consisted of a situation where demand, capital, and technology were given. Static conditions do change, however, over time: Populations grow, wants change, and improved production technologies are discovered and implemented. In other words, departures from static state equilibria are evolutionary. The mobility of labor and capital is requisite to the restoration of new, albeit temporary, equilibria. Clark's entrepreneur is the human agent responsible for the coordination that restores the economy to an equilibrium position. According to Clark, this coordinator may perform several functions.

> He may, for example, both labor and furnish capital, and he may, further, perform a special coordinating function which is not labor, in the technical sense, and scarcely involves any continuous personal activity at all, but is essential for rendering labor and

capital productive. We shall term [this] the function of the *entrepreneur*.* (1907, pp. 82-83)

This notion of the entrepreneur as the dynamic force that moves the economy back to equilibrium after some disturbance is still very much alive in contemporary theory, but it was soon to be challenged by Schumpeter's assertion that the entrepreneur is the agent that causes disequilibrium in the first place.

On the related matter of insurance, Clark (1892) recognized the differences between insurable and noninsurable risks (which he called "static" and "dynamic"), but he did not go so far as to integrate this distinction into a general theory that based profit on risk as well as dynamic change.

Hawley offered two rejoinders to Clark's criticism, one in 1893 and a summary statement seven years later designed to answer Clark and other critics who had joined the debate in the interim. In the second rejoinder Hawley proffered the view that "all individual incomes are composite, and that it is hard to imagine one that does not contain an element of profit and loss, as there is an element of uncertainty in the income of everybody" (1900, p. 78). In its time this was an unorthodox view, as it went against the prevailing tendency to compartmentalize distributional returns to factors of production. Yet it was particularly stimulating to academic economists who stubbornly resisted the idea that the theory of enterprise was a dark corner of economics that hid nothing of real importance.

The theme that engaged Hawley in the 1890s was picked up again by Knight in the 1920s and expanded into a full-blown theory of risk, uncertainty, and profit. But before Knight, the issue of entrepreneurship was also addressed by two fellow Americans, H. J. Davenport (1861-1931) and F. W. Taussig (1859-1940). Their ideas served to round out the backdrop for Knight's pioneering advance. Both Davenport (1913, p. 404) and Taussig considered entrepreneurial activity a special form of labor service, and both saw risk as inherent in entrepreneurial

---

*On the deficiencies of the argument that the entrepreneur is a mere coordinator, see Hawley (1900, pp. 84-89).

labor; however, neither regarded profit as necessarily proportionate to entrepreneurial risk.

Taussig declared that it was impracticable to separate even roughly the earnings of successful entrepreneurs into two parts — one "wages" and the other "profits" — the latter meaning gains from progress. Ironically, he considered, and rejected, the "Schumpeterian thesis" even before Schumpeter (see Chapter 7) made his views on entrepreneurship explicit and popular. Taussig's text is striking in this regard. We quote extensively from it here:

> One form . . . of dealing with the subject connects itself with . . . the consequences of changes in the arts. Business profits are treated as accruing solely from such changes. If changes in the arts were to cease, if competition were to work out its results perfectly, if prices were to conform closely to expenses of production, the managers of industry would receive nothing but wages — wages determined in the same fashion as other payments for labor. But in a dynamic state — a state of unstable equilibrium, of transition, of advance — there is opportunity for businessmen to secure something more. By taking the lead in utilizing inventions or improving organization they make extra gains, which last so long as they succeed in holding the lead. Business profits, so considered, are ever vanishing, ever reappearing. They are the stimulus to improvement and the reward for improvement, tending to cease when once the improvement is fully applied.
>
> The emphasis which this view puts on the relation between improvements and the businessman's gains is just. The large and conspicuous gains are in fact associated almost invariably with advances in the arts, with boldness and sagacity in exploiting new enterprises and new methods. None the less, this mode of sharply separating business profits from wages seems artificial. Even the routine conduct of established industries calls for judgment and administrative capacity, and so for the exercise of the same faculties that are more conspicuously and more profitably exercised under conditions of rapid progress. (1915, vol. II, p. 185)

In so many words, Taussig made clear a viewpoint that was to resurface again in the work of Mises (see Chapter 8), namely, that although innovation is one of the activities performed by the entrepreneur, it is not the only one, and perhaps not even the most important one.

Of all the American writers, however, the one to whom we owe the fullest and most careful examination of the role of the entrepreneur is Frank Knight (1885-1972), whose contribution was twofold. First, he provided a very useful emphasis on the distinction between insurable risks and noninsurable uncertainty. Second, he advanced a theory of profit that related this noninsurable uncertainty on the one hand to rapid economic change and on the other to differences in entrepreneurial ability. In so doing Knight established a meaningful synthesis of the Hawley-Clark formulations.

Knight charged that previous "risk theories" were ambiguous because they did not distinguish sufficiently between two very different kinds of risk. On the one hand, risk means a quantity capable of being measured, that is, the objective probability that an event will happen. Because this kind of risk can be shifted from the entrepreneur to another party by an insurance contract, it is not an uncertainty in any meaningful sense. On the other hand, "risk" is often taken to mean an unmeasurable unknown, such as the inability to predict consumer demand. Knight dubbed the latter "true" uncertainty and geared his theories of profit and entrepreneurship to its magnitude. The best summary statement of the theory comes from Knight himself:

> . . . not all "risks" necessarily give rise to profit, or loss. Many kinds can be *insured against*, which eliminates them as factors of uncertainty. . . . The essential point for profit theory is that insofar as it is possible to insure by any method against risk, the cost of carrying it is converted into a constant element of expense, and it ceases to be a cause of profit and loss.
>
> The uncertainties which persist as causes of profit are those which are uninsurable because there is no objective measure of the probability of gain or loss. This is true especially of the prediction of demand. It not only cannot be foreseen accurately, but there is no basis for saying that the probability of its being of one sort rather than another is of a certain value — as we can compute the chance that a man will live to a certain age. Situations in regard to which business judgment must be exercised do not repeat themselves with sufficient conformity to type to make possible a computation of probability. (1951, pp. 119-20)

Modern practice has refined Knight's distinction in the following way. Things once considered uninsurable because of lack of a measurable probability distribution have, in fact, been insured (for example, Liberace's fingers, Streisand's voice, Dolly Parton's bosom). Recent literature therefore makes three distinctions where Knight made two. Risk refers to the situation where the probability distribution of possible outcomes is calculable and known. Uncertainty refers to a situation where the possible outcomes are listable but the probability distribution of outcomes is not known. Radical uncertainty refers to a situation in which the possible outcomes of a given event are unknown and unlistable (because they are infinite).

Nevertheless, Knight's contribution offered a new refinement of Cantillon's theory of the entrepreneur as the bearer of uncertainty, because it isolated the concept of uncertainty and sharpened its meaning. Knight also added elements of economic evolution to his theory of enterprise. He asserted that the mere presence of uncertainty transforms society into an "enterprise organization" that is characterized by specialization of functions. The function of the entrepreneur becomes paramount in this kind of organization. According to Knight,

> Under the enterprise system, a special social class, the business men, direct economic activity; they are in the strict sense the producers, while the great mass of the population merely furnish them with productive services, placing their persons and their property at the disposal of this class; the entrepreneurs *also* guarantee to those who furnish productive services a fixed remuneration. (1921, p. 271)

This Knightian uncertainty is not easily compartmentalized, for it pervades all human decision making. But it helps establish a boundary between management and entrepreneurship. According to Knight (1921, p. 276), the function of manager does not in itself imply entrepreneurship, but a manager becomes an entrepreneur when his performance requires that he exercise judgment involving liability to error, and that a condition prerequisite to getting the other members of the firm to submit to his direction is his assumption of responsibility for the correctness of his judgments.

An interesting corollary of Knight's theory is that profit could not exist without error. Because entrepreneurial profit depends on whether an entrepreneur can make productive services yield more than the price fixed upon them by what other people think they can make them yield, its magnitude is therefore based on a margin of error in calculation by entrepreneurs and nonentrepreneurs who do not force the successful entrepreneurs to pay as much for productive services as they could be forced to pay. It is this margin of error in the faculty of judgment that constitutes the only true uncertainty in the workings of the competitive organization. Furthermore, it is this uncertainty that is borne by the true entrepreneur and explains profit in Knight's use of the term.

Knight commented on the separation of capitalist and entrepreneur, again falling back on the position taken centuries earlier by Cantillon. Both agreed that the entrepreneur may or may not be a capitalist — usually he must of necessity own some property, just as all property owners can hardly be freed from risk and responsibility. The point both writers stressed is that whether or not an entrepreneur owns capital the essence of entrepreneurship is not to be found therein. As Knight emphasized, "the only 'risk' which leads to [entrepreneurial] profit is a unique uncertainty resulting from an exercise of ultimate responsibility which in its very nature cannot be insured nor capitalized nor salaried" (1921, p. 310).

The range of possible activities undertaken by Knight's entrepreneur are wide indeed. One interesting idea along these lines has been expressed recently by Donald Schon (1963, p. 84). Schon portrays the entrepreneur as a champion of new ideas and technologies, willing to "put himself on the line for an idea of doubtful success," accepting the risk of failure. He sees the entrepreneur as a kind of "broker" of new technologies, noting that "technological innovation requires leaps that cannot be justified before the fact by those charged with the task. So, there comes into being a man who takes the burden of risk on his shoulders without formal justification . . . , entrepreneurs without authority" (1976, p. 118).

Jay Forrester (1965), however, cautions that today's entrepreneur gets but one chance to succeed — a dubious assertion, but one seconded by Modesto Maidique (1980). Not all economists have found Knight's formulation appropriate. Fritz Redlich (1957) contends that Knight's theory is of no use to the historian of entrepreneurship because it offers no distinction between ownership and control, on the one hand, and management and decision making, on the other.

Despite the diversity of theories of entrepreneurship surveyed to this point, they all share the common point of view that entrepreneurial activity is a response to some exogenous force exerted on the market system. The first truly radical departure from this overweening perspective was taken by an economist who etched his name in the annals of economics by declaring the entrepreneur to be an endogenous factor and something of a mischief maker to boot. That person was Schumpeter, whose views on the entrepreneur are the subject of the next chapter.

CHAPTER 7

THE ENTREPRENEUR
RECONSTITUTED

The carrying out of new combinations we call "enterprise"; the individuals whose function it is to carry them out we call "entrepreneurs."

J. A. Schumpeter

The writers surveyed in the previous chapter worked within the equilibrium tradition of mainstream economics. In its neoclassical form, economic theory has been primarily concerned with the pricing of a collection of goods and services, the unknown of the problem being determined by the requisite number of givens in each situation. In such cases, uncertainty, in the sense of the incalculable, has no meaning. A solution to the problem requires that the actual and the calculable coincide. Deviations of one from the other, such as true uncertainty allows, cannot be admitted. Thus, Maurice Dobb correctly asserts that "in a system of economic equilibrium the work of the entrepreneur cannot be qualitatively different from that of any other agent of production" (1937, p. 559).

To postulate a true functional theory of entrepreneurship, there must be some potential within the analytic model for the entrepreneur to engage in decision making that alters the equilibrium position of the enterprise. As seen in the last chapter, a tentative step in this direction was taken by Clark. Clark was an American economist, but he was trained by Knies in the tradition of the German historical school. This chapter begins with a discussion of the German historicists and then links their writings to Schumpeter. It is with Schumpeter that a more complete dynamic theory of the entrepreneur as an innovator first developed.

THE GERMAN HISTORICAL SCHOOL

The development of economic thought in the late nineteenth and early twentieth centuries progressed quite differently in Germany than it did in England or in France. This was due in part to the methodological influence of the German historical movement. The historicists believed that in order to understand man's economic behavior and the institutions that constrain such behavior, it is necessary to describe man's motives and behavioral tendencies in psychologically realistic terms. Man is not a "hedonistic atom," and his economic behavior cannot fully be described in individualistic terms (Spengler and Allen 1960).

At the outset, there were three major forces within the German historical movement – Wilhelm Roscher (1817-1894), Karl Knies (1821-1898), and Bruno Hildebrand (1812-1878). Their writings represent a reaction against received economics. It was their contention that a thorough analysis and complete understanding of historical data were prerequisites for proper development of any economic theory.

Gustav Schmöller (1838-1917) typifies the second generation of historicists. Reacting against Ricardian doctrine, Schmöller began to analyze actual (historical) economic behavior, and as he did so, he began to discover a unique central factor present in all economic activity. This factor was the enterprising spirit, the *Unternehmer*, or the entrepreneur. The entrepreneur was seen as a creative organizer and manager whose role was innovation and initiation (Zrinyi 1962).

Schmöller's entrepreneur combined factors of production to yield either new productive processes or new products. He is, therefore, much more than an undertaker involved in routine affairs. He must be imaginative and bold, quite like Wieser's entrepreneur.

Werner Sombart (1863-1941) and Max Weber (1864-1920) are third-generation historicists who extended Schmöller's ideas. Sombart introduced a "new leader" who animates the entire economic system via creative innovation. First, the entrepreneur is an organizer, much like Schmöller's entrepreneur, but he is also more than that. In addition to combining creatively factors of production in order to obtain maximum profits (for the enterprise and for himself), he must have the personality and ability to temper individuals in order to obtain from them maximum productivity. Zrinyi's interpretation of Sombart captures these aspects exceedingly well:

> Different situations and talents may develop different types of entrepreneurs. Financiers, traders, manufacturers of new commodities or organizers of new processes of production are the different facets of entrepreneurial activities. (1962, p. 73)

In the tradition of the German historicists, the entrepreneur was to accomplish these goals by breaking away from the old methods of production and creating new ones. This disequilibrating notion was particularly emphasized by Weber. His task was to explain how a social system (note the unit of analysis is no longer the individual enterprise) could evolve from one stable form (perhaps under an authoritarian structure) to another type of system. Historically such changes have always been associated with some "charismatic leader" — an entrepreneurial-like notion (Carlin 1956).

Weber began his analysis with a stationary-state construct:

> We may thus visualize an economic process which merely reproduces itself at constant rates; a given population, not changing in either numbers or age distribution. . . . The tasks (wants) of

households are given and do not change. The ways of production and usances of commerce are optimal from the standpoint of the firm's interest and with respect to existing horizons and possibilities, hence do not change either, unless some datum changes or some chance event intrudes upon this world. (1930, p. 67)

In such a stationary society there is nothing that requires the activity traditionally associated with the entrepreneur. "No other than ordinary routine work has to be done in this stationary society, either by workmen or managers" (Weber 1930, p. 67).

At some point, however, this tranquil, self-perpetuating state will be altered:

Now at some time this leisureliness was suddenly destroyed, and often entirely without any essential change in form of organization. . . . What happened was, on the contrary, often no more than this: Some young man from one of the putting-out families went out into the country, carefully chose weavers from his employ, greatly increased the rigour of his supervision of their work, and thus turned them from peasants into laborours. . . . [H]e would begin to change his marketing methods. . . . [H]e began to introduce the principle of low prices and large turnover. There was repeated what everywhere and always is the result of such a process of rationalization: those who would not follow suit had to go out of business. The idyllic state collapsed under the pressure of a bitter competitive struggle. . . . (1930, p. 68)

The motives behind this entrepreneurial force are important for a complete understanding of Weber's sociological theory. For Weber, the critical characteristics of the successful entrepreneur are his religious imperatives. These imperatives make up what is called the Protestant ethic.

SCHUMPETER'S CONTRIBUTION

Schumpeter (1883-1950) represents an integrating figure in the history of entrepreneurial thought. He succeeded in integrating the dynamics of technology and business enterprise. There are distinctive philosophical elements in Schumpeter's thought connecting him with the German historical school, and there are elements reflecting his awareness and understanding of the process of evolution that occurs in all capitalistic societies (Zrinyi 1962). Somewhat paradoxically, he was also a professed admirer of the French economist Leon Walras.

As a starting point for describing Schumpeter's entrepreneur, it is important to understand the general economic setting that the entrepreneur enters. It is also important to realize that the Schumpeterian entrepreneur is a construct, much like Weber's "charismatic leader," which is introduced to disrupt the "self-perpetuating equilibrium."

Schumpeter's model presents "the fundamental facts and relations of economic life in their simplest form" (1939, pp. 13-14). His starting point is the concept of circular flow, "an unchanging economic process which flows on at constant rates in time and merely reproduces itself" (1939, p. 13). This equilibrium process is posited within a closed economic system. Schumpeter set forth the characteristics of this system as follows:

> A given population, not changing in either numbers or age distribution, organized for purposes of consumption in households and for purposes of production and trade in firms, lives and works in an unchanging physical and social (institutional) environment. The tastes (wants) of households are given and do not change. The ways of production and usances of commerce are optional from the standpoint of the firm's interest and with respect to existing horizons and possibilities, hence do not change either, unless some datum changes or some chance event intrudes upon this world. (1939, p. 15)

Within this system, the production function is invariant; however, factor substitutability is possible within the limits of known technological horizons. Beyond the task of resource allocation "[n]o other than ordinary routine work has to be done . . . in fact . . . beyond this there is . . . no managerial function — nothing that calls for the special type of activity which we associate with the entrepreneur" (Schumpeter 1939,

p. 17). In other words, in the circular flow the entrepreneur "simply does not exist,"* and managers are reduced to mere choreographers of economic activity. They "direct" their own work routines and those of other workers in a purely perfunctory fashion (Schumpeter 1961, pp. 76, 84).

This circular flow idea is a theoretical construct that describes a system's tendency to move or grope toward equilibrium (in this sense it is akin to Walras's *tâtonnement*). A final equilibrium is never fully obtained in the circular flow. Data do change, however, and the circular flow can adjust to discrete or to continuous changes in social and nonsocial data.

ENTREPRENEURS AND INNOVATION

In reality, societies and their environments do not change in discrete steps. "Revolutionary" changes occur and manifest themselves in "new combinations" of the factors of production. The adoption of new combinations is in itself a creative response as it represents the assimilation of knowledge not yet in current use. The consequences of these new combinations are innovation – the "setting up of a new production function" (Schumpeter 1939, p. 62). Schumpeter actually defined innovation by means of the production function:

> . . . This function describes the way in which quantity of product varies if quantities of factors vary. If, instead of quantities of factors, we vary the form of the function, we have an innovation. (1939, p. 62)

This innovation must consist of producing and marketing a new commodity; otherwise the innovation would represent a cost-reducing adaptation of knowledge, which leads only to a new supply schedule. Schumpeter pointed out quite clearly that this knowledge underlying the innovation need not be

---

*What the writers in Chapter 6 described as the role of the entrepreneur, Schumpeter would have simply labeled as managerial activity. The entrepreneur does not take on a personality until the economic system moves out of the routineness of a continual equilibrium.

newly discovered — it may be existing knowledge that has never been utilized in production:

> [T] here never has been anytime when the store of scientific knowledge has yielded all it could in the way of industrial improvement, and, on the other hand, it is not the knowledge that matters, but the *successful* [emphasis added] solution of the task *sui generis* of putting an untried method into practice — there may be, and often is, no scientific novelty involved at all, and even if it be involved, this does not make any difference to the nature of the process. (1928, p. 378)

What makes the task of innovation, or more precisely, successful innovation a task sui generis? For Schumpeter, successful innovation requires an act of will, not of intellect. It therefore depends on leadership and not mere intelligence.

As it relates to innovation, leadership is a heterogeneous characteristic. It refers in part to a power to make use of knowledge. To an extent, knowledge is a public good, but those in positions of management perceive and react to it in various ways. Schumpeter noted:

> Whilst differences in aptitude for the routine work of "static" management only results in differences of success in doing what everyone does, differences in [leadership] aptitude result in only some being able to [undertake] uncertainties incident to what has not been done before. . . . To overcome these difficulties incident to change of practice is the function of the entrepreneur. (1928, p. 380)

This kind of entrepreneurial leadership is less glamorous than other forms of leadership but is held to be no less important by Schumpeter.

Schumpeter's entrepreneurial function contrasts sharply with the managerial function described by Mill, but it is not so dissimilar to Marshall's entrepreneur, who is always on the lookout for new methods of production. Accordingly, like Marshall, Schumpeter makes the entrepreneur's profits distinct from the earnings of management. Schumpeter (1928) noted that individual fortunes have been built on entrepreneurial profits, but he did not come right out and suggest that the potential for these profits is the primary incentive for the emergence of entrepreneurial talent. Thus it is the entrepreneur, through his workings within the economic system, who motivates the capitalistic process. This will occur whether or not there are exogenous factors impinging on the growth process. The entrepreneur is unequivocably an endogenous force in the Schumpeterian system.

In his later writings Schumpeter saw the innovation process as the precursor to economic development:*

> Development . . . is a distinct phenomenon, entirely foreign to what may be observed in the circular flow or in the tendency towards equilibrium. It is a spontaneous and discontinuous change in the channels of the flow, disturbance of equilibrium, which forever alters and displaces the equilibrium state previously existing. [The] theory of development is nothing but a treatment of this phenomenon and the process incident to it. (1961, p. 64)

In the context of economic development, Schumpeter saw fit to widen the definition of the entrepreneur to include anyone, within a firm or not, who carries out new combinations. These new combinations constitute "enterprise," the mobilization of resources for production. Thus after a long time, Schumpeter vested economics with a highly refined role for the entrepreneur, one that treats the entrepreneur as an endogenous rather than an exogenous factor. His "new" concept eventually became the prototype for subsequent treatments of the human agent in the theory of economic development.

From a pragmatic perspective, a functional entrepreneur needs to exercise more than the "creative" dimension of his personality. Schumpeter stressed only the creative component of the entrepreneur in his theory of economic development; however, more contemporary writers have realized that the "cooperative" component is equally important. According to Albert O. Hirschman, for example, a functional entrepreneur

---

*According to Adrien Taymans (1949), the locus of this idea of dynamic development expressed by Schumpeter is to be found in the earlier work of George Tarde (1834-1904), the French sociologist.

must be more than a Schumpeterian "rebel against society." He must embody the "ability to engineer *agreement* [emphasis added] among all interested parties, such as the inventor of the [new] process, the partner, the capitalist, the supplier of parts and services, the distributors, etc." (1958, p. 17). In developing countries, the focus of Hirschman's interest, there must be a balance of the creative and cooperative components if growth is to ensue.

It is especially noteworthy that Schumpeter regarded his conception as historically legitimate, while he simultaneously excluded risk from his purview of the entrepreneur. On this, Schumpeter was quite explicit:

> I maintain that [this] definition does no more than formulate with greater precision what the traditional doctrine really means to convey. In this first place [the] definition agrees with the usual one on the fundamental point of distinguishing between "entrepreneurs" and "capitalists" — irrespective of whether the latter are regarded as owners of money, claims to money, or material goods. . . . It also settles the question whether the ordinary shareholder as such is an entrepreneur, and disposes the conception of the entrepreneur as risk bearer. . . . Risk obviously always falls on the owner of the means of production or of the money-capital which was paid for them, hence never on the entrepreneur *as such*. (1961, p. 75)

CONTRASTS AND CONFLICTS

Schumpeter's influence on subsequent entrepreneurial theory has been enormous, even among those economists who reject the theory outright and those who have set about to modify it. Despite many superficial similarities on this subject by Schumpeter and Weber, Schumpeter's vision has proven to be more appealing to economists over the long haul. Ronan Macdonald (1971) has analyzed this circumstance and concludes that the difference lies largely in what each man made of his vision. Weber saw in the innovator the "ideal type" of the Protestant worldly ascetic. Schumpeter, on the other hand, chose to regard him as the supernormal entrepreneur. This was a distinct analytic advance, because in a theory of economic evolution it is more plausible to postulate the appearance of men of extraordinary ability as causes of change than to postulate the appearance of Calvin or some other charismatic figure. At base, Schumpeter's theory of the entrepreneur is a theory of economic leadership, and, unlike Weber's, it does not invoke any extraeconomic elements. Schumpeter's system very tidily hinges on three corresponding pairs of opposites: the circular flow and the developing economy, statics and dynamics, and the entrepreneur versus the mere manager.

As a theory of economic change, Schumpeter's theory occupies the middle ground between the theories of Marshall and Weber. Marshall's system adapted incrementally to shifts in preference and production functions, the result being a continuous improvement in moral qualities, tastes, and economic techniques. Its shortcoming was that it admitted no business cycles, a deficiency that Marshall's student Keynes set about to repair. Marshall's approach also implied a theory of unilinear evolution, which Schumpeter's vision denied. Moreover, Weber's theory explained rapid social and economic transitions punctuating long periods of historical continuity, whereas Schumpeter postulated the continuous occurrence of innovations and waves of adaptation, because entrepreneurs are always present (Macdonald 1971).

Schumpeter's entrepreneur is obviously a person of unusual will and energy. But he is also a person with no capital. In this connection, Schumpeter broke sharply with his teacher Böhm-Bawerk, for whom the entrepreneur was clearly the capitalist and there was no possibility of such separation. This sharp cleavage between the two led Schumpeter to Clark's idiosyncratic position that "the entrepreneur is never the risk bearer" (1961, p. 137). It also raised the broader question of the role of uncertainty in the world of entrepreneurial decisions. It is on these two points rather than his central vision that Schumpeter's theory has been subject to the most scrutiny.

Whereas Hawley was Clark's chief antagonist on this issue of risk, the most recent criticism of Schumpeter's systematic exclusion of risk bearing from the entrepreneurial function was provided by Kanbur (1980), whose view on this subject was stated briefly in Chapter 3. Kanbur criticized Schumpeter for being myopic to the point of disregarding other forms of risk besides mere financial risk. He introduced opportunity cost as a factor in determining entrepreneurial risk, especially for the noncapitalist. Kanbur maintains that both capital risk and entrepreneurial risk exist, whereas Schumpeter only recognized the former. Entrepreneurial risk can be identified by examining the decision to supply capital and direct the enterprise versus the decision merely to supply capital. In Kanbur's terms:

> The individual need not run the enterprise himself. Indeed, part of the uncertainty facing him may well arise from self-doubt as to his *ability* as entrepreneur. This uncertainty could be circumvented by lending his capital to somebody who could offer a better distribution of returns, while himself taking up employment in which he is less uncertain of his ability. Those who do not do so "risk their reputation," at least in relation to the safe alternative, as well as risking their capital. The two risks can indeed be separated out for conceptual or analytical purposes, not least because the opportunity cost of the capital will, in general, be different from the opportunity cost of entrepreneurial effort, and it is relative to these opportunity costs that gains and losses, and hence risks, have to be conceptualized. (1980, p. 493)

In an earlier paper, Kanbur (1979) found the Cantillon-Knight formulation more amenable to the task of modeling entrepreneurial behavior, especially for the purpose of discovering the relationship between risk taking and personal income distribution.

Schumpeter's denial of risk as an element of entrepreneurship raises anew the question of the role of uncertainty in the dynamic economy. Schumpeter cited the changing character of the entrepreneur:

> [T]he entrepreneur's essential function must always appear mixed up with other kinds of activity, which as a rule must be more conspicuous than the essential one. . . . [E]veryone is an entrepreneur only when he actually "carries out new combinations," and loses that character as soon as he has built up his business, when he settles down to running it as other people run their business. (1961, pp. 77-78)

This changing character of the entrepreneur suggests that his return for introducing new combinations is not a permanent return. Genuinely innovative decisions must certainly be shrouded with uncertainty, and pure entrepreneurial gain would only exist if the entrepreneur's decisions are successful in situations of uncertainty.

Andreas Papandreau (1943) avers that the element of uncertainty is downplayed by Schumpeter but that it is crucial to an understanding and appreciation of the environment in which entrepreneurs break away from the routine. To offset this, Papandreau posited an alternative definition that makes uncertainty explicit: "The entrepreneur would be the one who carries out innovation under conditions of uncertainty and unpredictability" (1943, p. 23).

CHAPTER 8

THE ENTREPRENEUR
EXTENDED

The question of how the business man's mind works and what materials it works with in approaching a decision . . . is one of the most fascinating . . . in the whole of economics.

G. L. S. Shackle

The essence of the entrepreneurial decision consists in *grasping* the knowledge that might otherwise remain unexploited.

I. M. Kirzner

Much of the twentieth-century literature about the entrepreneur and entrepreneurship has emanated from Schumpeter's theory of innovation and his view of the entrepreneur within the innovation process. But contemporary writers have reacted to Schumpeter in different ways. One school seems to have accepted the Schumpeterian exposition and concerned itself chiefly with a methodological approach to studying the entrepreneur and his role. Some writers have rejected Schumpeter's characterization of the entrepreneur as a disequilibrating factor,

85

portraying him instead as an equilibrating force. Still others have embellished earlier visions of the entrepreneur with their own particular refinements.

In this chapter we survey some of these contemporary views. In general, two broad traditions have been at work; one centered on a group of Harvard economists, the other a prodigy of the Austrian school. We portray the former as an extension of the Schumpeterian view, whereas the latter is represented as an alternative. Our purpose here is not to reconcile these approaches, but to examine different strands woven into the contemporary economic fabric. Individual contributions of major import are also considered, notably those of G. L. S. Shackle and Theodore W. Schultz.

THE HARVARD TRADITION

The so-called Harvard tradition refers not so much to a new theory of entrepreneurship as to a methodological approach to the study of the topic. Still, some interesting and useful definitions of entrepreneurship have come from this group of writers. The methodology of this school is primarily based on the ideas generated at the Research Center in Entrepreneurial History at Harvard University, which was founded by Cole (1889-1974). Cole's views developed, in part, from his association with Edwin F. Gay (1867-1946), founder and first president of the Economic History Association, whose interest in the entrepreneur stemmed from his filiation with Schumpeter. In fact, the entrepreneur (viewed as a disequilibrating agent in the manner of Schumpeter) played an important role in Gay's philosophy of history, which asserts that the amount of permissible free competition existing in society varies with the social need. In this system of free competition the entrepreneur is a self-centered actor and a disruptive force, but according to Gay, "there are periods in the rhythm of history when . . . that disruptive, innovating energy is socially advantageous and must be given freer opportunity" (1923-24, p. 12).

Following this lead, Cole insisted that the entrepreneur's role in economic activity had been neglected. To him, the entrepreneur is not only the central figure in modern economic history; he is as well the central figure in economics. In order to discover the uniqueness of entrepreneurship and its importance to economics, Cole advocated an approach that includes case studies of the entrepreneur in business history, cross-sectional investigations of particular individuals who exercise entrepreneurial talents over time, longitudinal studies of specific entrepreneurial functions (such as trends in personnel policies), and conceptual studies in historico-entrepreneurship that may also be used to draw solutions to current problems.*

Cole's entrepreneur has two notable features. First, he is a productive agent who utilizes other productive factors for the creation of goods. Second, he makes decisions under uncertainty. In what was the most comprehensive (if not wordy) definition of entrepreneurship since Wieser, Cole stated:

> Entrepreneurship may be defined as the purposeful activity (including an integrated sequence of decisions) of an individual or group of associated individuals, undertaken to initiate, maintain, or aggrandize a profit-oriented business unit for the production or distribution of economic goods and services with pecuniary or other advantage the goal or measure of success, in interaction with (or within the conditions established by) the internal situation of the unit itself or with the economic, political, and social circumstances (institutions and practices) of a period which allows an appreciable measure of freedom of decision. (1949, p. 88)

"Purposeful activity" is potentially a multifarious concept. We take it to mean that entrepreneurial activity is directed toward some goal, presumably profit maximization. It may also refer to the rational ability to make decisions and to an ability to implement these decisions.† "An integrated sequence of

---

*See also, Karl Deutsch (1949), who outlined a functional analysis of the study of entrepreneurship resembling Cole's. Deutsch suggested that one first identify the single, most important technical or social function performed by the entrepreneur, then investigate this function (as well as its secondary effects) with respect to a particular time and place.

†Hugh G. J. Aitken (1949) stressed parameters in the entrepreneur's environment, such as technological advances in technical knowledge, which influence his decision-making abilities.

decisions" suggests the importance of an organization (presumably formal) in the conceptual understanding of entrepreneurship, a theme amplified by Leland H. Jenks.* The "business unit" as an institutional datum therefore constitutes the basis for a theory of entrepreneurial action in this view. According to Jenks

> Business unit and entrepreneur are interdependent conceptions. A business unit consists in a system of entrepreneurial and nonentrepreneurial roles structured as a system of exchange sets, productive performers, and co-operative activities. (1949, p. 151)

This quotation typifies one theme of the Harvard school, namely, that a functional definition or understanding of the entrepreneur is meaningless unless it is associated with environmental characteristics that influence the entrepreneur's decision-making process. It is interesting to compare this viewpoint with that of Schumpeter, who perceived that the innovative actions of the entrepreneur also impact upon the environment in a symbiotic fashion.

This particular notion of the entrepreneur as decision maker prevails today in many management-related academic studies. For example, William Souder (1981, p. 18) views research and development as one arena in which the entrepreneur guides and champions successful projects. Such individuals, "influenced by emotion and intuition," take risks by making "quick decisions" on a limited number of facts. In line with the Harvard school theme, Souder suggests that firms do not foster an environment that encourages or enhances entrepreneurial activities. The reason is quite pragmatic: Firms are engaged in active competition and accordingly tend to pursue conservative, proven approaches to new ventures.

---

*Elsewhere, Cole (1959) has stated that entrepreneurship is really a plural concept. Evans (1949) and Spengler (1949) also stressed this point. Spengler suggests that one could conceive of a set of tasks that needs to be done and is done (by an entrepreneurial group) as the entrepreneurial function. See also Strauss (1944) and Schon (1976), who suggest that the firm be viewed as the entrepreneur.

SHACKLE'S IMPACT

Over the last three decades, in a number of seminal works, one writer in particular, Shackle, has made the psychic act of decision in the world of enterprise the chief focus of his interest. In investigating the nature and essence of business enterprise, Shackle (1955) identified two roles that must be performed. One is bearing uncertainty; the other is making decisions. These two roles are not unrelated, as decision making means to improvise or invent — actions that are genuinely possible only in a world of unknowns and uncertainties.

Shackle is at his best in explicating the nature of business decisions and the scope for human action within them. An astute Marshallian, he is critical of mainstream economic theory for its failure to recognize the full implications of time in the world of affairs. In Shackle's view the problem with which time confronts us in economic analysis is essentially this:

How to find a scheme of thought about the basic nature of human affairs, which will include *decision* in the meaning we give to this word in our unselfconscious, intuitive, instinctive attitude to life, where without examination or heart-searching we take it for granted that a responsibility lies upon us for our acts; that these acts are in a profound sense *creative, inceptive*, the source of *historical novelty*; that each such act is, as it were, the unconnected starting point of a new thread in the tapestry which time is weaving. (1966, p. 73)

This view places considerable pressure on economic modes of thought, for it requires that uncertainty be squarely faced, that deterministic models be rejected, but that some sort of order nevertheless obtain in the world of practical affairs. In sum, the territory carved out by Shackle includes the reconciliation of uncertainty and imaginative experience. It is these two elements that make up every business decision. But what is uncertainty? Shackle defines it as a state of mind, something subjective. This subjective magnitude is nevertheless bound by possibility, which is important in order to keep the problem under investigation within the scope of analytic manipulation. Shackle speaks directly to this point:

If a man can set no bounds to what may follow upon any act of his own, he evidently looks upon himself as powerless to affect the course of events. There are, indeed, two views of history which would compel him to acknowledge his own powerlessness. If history is determinate, he cannot alter its predestinate course. If history is anarchy and randomness, he cannot modify this randomness nor mitigate the orderlessness of events. It is only a *bounded* uncertainty that will permit him to act creatively. (1966, p. 86)

In Shackle's paradigm, uncertainty means plurality of rival hypotheses regarding outcomes of a given action. Each outcome is considered to be mutually exclusive, yet not impossible. For its part, decision means (1) the pursuit of imaginative experience and (2) choice in the face of bounded uncertainty. Most of Shackle's work has aimed at elaborating the second element of this definition. Those individuals who make decisions of the kind Shackle describes are called "enterprisers." Shackle is justified in choosing this term in preference to the more ambiguous term of entrepreneur, yet there is little discernible difference between his enterpriser and Cantillon's entrepreneur. Indeed, in the following passage, Shackle is strongly evocative of Cantillon's distinction between those who live on "fixed wages" and those who "buy at a certain price and sell at an uncertain price" (see Chapter 3):

Uncertainty is inherent in production, but it does not follow that all who take part in it need bear uncertainty; those who wish can contract out of uncertainty. Let us assume that money is regarded by everyone as an unchanging standard of value. Then if, amongst all those who intend to contribute the services of themselves or of their property to the making of some exchangeable thing, some agree to accept from the others a stated money payment and to surrender to these others all their rights in the product, we can say that at the date when these contracts are made the planned operation has two quite different meanings for the two groups of producers. To one group it means an income of known size, for the other group it means the unknown difference between the total of the contractual payments and the price for which the product will exchange. Let us treat this second group as a single person and call him the enterpriser, and let us ascribe to him both of the two roles . . . , that of decision-maker and that of uncertainty bearer. Then what induces him to venture on production is something essentially different in character from what induces the recipients of contractual incomes to furnish their services. (1955, pp. 82-83)

What is more important, however, is that Shackle has attempted to move beyond Cantillon's original conception. Not content merely to emphasize the entrepreneur's role, Shackle has attempted to get inside his head in order to discover the basis of enterprising decisions. The fact that Shackle has sought to integrate fully the effects of time into the economics of decision making, or that his approach is both subjective and psychological* does not, in our opinion, place him outside the Cantillon tradition.

One feature of Shackle's analysis that does place him at the outer edge of mainstream economics is his disregard for the equilibrium method. Shackle sees his own work as an offshoot of a Keynesian concern, namely, the determinants of business investment. Yet he detects a fundamental inconsistency in the Keynesian paradigm. Of the *General Theory*, Shackle has remarked, "The book is a paradox, for its central concern is with uncertainty, decisions based on conjecture, and situations altogether lacking in objective stability, yet it uses an equilibrium method" (1955, p. 222). By contrast, Shackle discards the equilibrium method, and this fact most probably accounts for the failure of mainstream economics to take his analysis more seriously. Still, Shackle has his followers, most particularly Ludwig Lachman, who also has at least one foot in the Austrian camp.

NEO-AUSTRIAN VIEWS

Of the nineteenth-century triumvirate that constituted the Austrian school in economics (see Chapter 6), it was Wieser

---

*At one point, Shackle unequivocally stated, "Economics is not physics, it is psychics, the study of men with all their capacity for learning and experimenting and inventing and imagining" (1955, p. 235).

who extended Menger's insights about the entrepreneur, investing him with the qualities of leadership, alertness, and risk bearing, and theorizing that entrepreneurial action impacts upon society as a whole and not just on the enterprise. Although Böhm-Bawerk's direct contributions to a functional theory of entrepreneurship were minimal, both Schumpeter and Mises (1881-1972) were students of his at the University of Vienna. We shall see, however, that their respective theories of entrepreneurship are miles apart.

In order to place the modern Austrian ideas about entrepreneurship in proper perspective, it is first necessary to discuss Mises's concept of human action. Like Clark and Schumpeter, who developed their theories by first introducing artificial constructs of the economy – the static state, the circular flow – and then hypothesizing how entrepreneurial activity alters these states, Mises constructed the concept of an "evenly rotating economy" free from change, in order to contrast it with one in which change occurs. The evenly rotating economy represents a rigid picture of the world – a world characterized by the elimination of change in data and time, a world of perfect price stability where market prices and final prices coincide. In such a setting human behavior can be nothing more than involuntary response: "[T]his system is not peopled with living men making choices and liable to error; it is a world of soulless unthinking automatons; it is not a human society, it is an ant hill" (Mises 1949, p. 249). Once human action is viewed as "purposeful behavior," changes will occur; according to Mises, "Action is change."*

A fundamental characteristic of Mises's human action is that it influences a future state of affairs. Thus "the outcome of action is always uncertain. Action is always speculation" (1949, p. 253). Consequently, participants in a changing economy make choices and cope with the subsequent uncertainties

---

*Mises justifies the construction of the evenly rotating economy in the following manner: "There is no means of studying the complex phenomena of action other than first to abstract from change altogether, then to introduce an isolated factor provoking change, and ultimately to analyze its effects under the assumption that other things remain equal" (1949, pp. 248-49).

of the future. In such an economy "the term entrepreneur . . . means . . . acting man exclusively seen from the aspect of uncertainty inherent in every action" (1949, p. 254). Given this functional definition, it is clear that in the evenly rotating system no one is an entrepreneur. But in the more realistic dynamic economy, "every actor is always an entrepreneur" (1949, p. 253). Capitalists who lend their assets with less than perfect certainty regarding repayment are entrepreneurs.* Farmers, too, are entrepreneurs — in fact, no proprietor of any factor of production is untouched by the uncertainty of the future. Laborers are entrepreneurs insofar as wages are determined by uncertain market activities.

At base, the only observable difference between the notion of the entrepreneur presented by Mises and that drawn by Cantillon is that Mises cast an even wider net, bringing into his definition the landowners and laborers that Cantillon excluded. Mises therefore may be said to have democratized Cantillon's concept. Otherwise, both formulations share the function of bearing uncertainty.

In developing his concept of entrepreneurship, Mises had an eye to a functional share of income distribution. He admitted that the term entrepreneur refers to an imaginary figure. It applies not to a man or group of men but to a function, one that "is inherent in every action and burdens every actor" (1949, p. 253), a function animated by the prospect of gain. Mises was aware, however, of the ambiguous nature of the term in contemporary use. He observed:

> Economics . . . also calls entrepreneurs those who are especially eager to profit from adjusting production to the expected changes in conditions, those who have more initiative, more venturesomeness, and a quicker eye than the crowd, the pushing and promoting pioneers of economic development. This notion is narrower than the concept of an entrepreneur as used in the construction of functional distribution; it does not include many instances which the latter includes. It is awkward that the same term

---

*Mises is, however, adamant that this does not imply that entrepreneurs must also be capitalists.

should be used to signify two different notions. It would have been more expedient to employ another term for this second notion — for instance, the term "promoter." (1949, pp. 254-55)

Mises took some pains to distinguish his conception of the entrepreneur from Schumpeter's. Referring to "the errors due to the confusion of entrepreneurial activity and technological innovation and improvement," Mises declared:

> Changes in the data, especially in consumers' demand, may require adjustments which have no reference at all to techno-logical innovations and improvements. . . . The business of the entrepreneur is not merely to experiment with new technological methods, but to select from the multitude of technologically feasible methods those which are best fit to supply the public in the cheapest way with the things they are asking for most urgently. Whether a new technological procedure is or is not fit for this purpose is to be provisionally decided by the entre-preneur and will be finally decided by the conduct of the buying public. (1951, p. 11)

Clearly, for Mises "the activities of the entrepreneur consist in making decisions" (1951, p. 12), and while decisions regard-ing innovation and technological improvement come under his purview, such decisions alone do not constitute an exhaus-tive set.

The contrast between Schumpeter and Mises becomes more poignant if we approach their differences from the standpoint of the theory of economic growth. Schumpeter's growth theory is closely tied to the innovative activities of the entrepreneur, who creates opportunities for economic growth and thereby assures that the process is ongoing. But every new innovation requires capital to give it life, which presupposes some level of real saving and its unhampered movement toward investment opportunities. Schumpeter saw the level of real saving as a necessary but not a sufficient condition for economic growth. He argued that innovation was needed to mobilize idle savings. Thus the binding constraints in the Schumpeterian system are the quantity and quality of new innovations. By contrast, Mises considered real saving to be both the necessary and sufficient condition for economic growth. It is the level of real saving that underwrites every profit opportunity, but profit opportunities are not limited to new innovations. Clearly, without real saving even the most promising innovations will remain inoperative. The binding constraint in Mises's theory of economic growth is therefore the level of real saving.

Closely connected to the theory of economic growth is the fact that profit and loss are the carrot and stick of entrepreneurial activity. "It is the entrepreneurial decision that creates either profit or loss," argued Mises (1951, p. 21), not capital, as Marx thought. Capital can be used according to good or bad (mistaken) ideas. If utilized according to a good idea, profit results. "It is mental acts, the mind of the entrepreneur, from which profits ultimately originate. Profit is a product of the mind, of success in anticipating the future state of the market."

One of the most provocative of the "new" theories of entrepreneurship has been put forward recently by Israel Kirzner who was a student of Mises at New York University. Like Shackle, Kirzner argues that the equilibrium method of economic analysis has done much mischief because it leaves no room for purposeful human action. But Kirzner refuses to ride in the same coach as Shackle, who denies that the economic system necessarily harbors a tendency toward equilibrium, a view manifestly too radical for Kirzner's tastes. Indeed, for Kirzner the role of the entrepreneur is to achieve the kind of adjustment necessary to move economic markets toward the equilibrium state. This crucial role is overlooked, Kirzner contends, by economic models that focus on equilibrium results rather than the process by which equilibrium is attained.

Kirzner maintains that in traditional neoclassical economic models, "[e]quilibrium simply means a state in which each decision correctly anticipates all other decisions" (1979a, p. 110). By the neoclassical method, decisions are made and actions taken by mere mechanical calculations; judgment has no place; each market participant makes decisions that merely adjust given means to suit a given end (Kirzner 1973). But in the Misesian (dynamic) economy, knowledge is never complete or perfect; therefore, markets are constantly in states of disequilibrium, and it is disequilibrium that gives scope to the entrepreneurial function. It is the entrepreneur's job to remove maladjustments that bar the return to equilibrium (Mises 1951, p. 11).

In his own formulation of entrepreneurship, Kirzner gave the impression of departing from Mises in several subtle ways, thereby drawing the fire of otherwise friendly critics. Objection has been raised to Kirzner's belief in a "pure and penniless" entrepreneur, that is, one who does not own any capital. It has been pointed out by neo-Austrians in general that if one has nothing to lose there is no sense in which he can be said to bear risk, which is the essence of Mises's concept of entrepreneurship. For example, Mises noted: "There is a simple rule of thumb to tell entrepreneurs from non-entrepreneurs. The entrepreneurs are those on whom the incidence of losses on the capital employed falls" (1951, p. 13). Kirzner has maintained that the essence of entrepreneurship consists in the alertness of market participants to profit opportunities and that the full implications of this notion have not been made explicit by either Wieser or Mises, in whose works the idea resides.

In his lectures Kirzner likes to stress the analogy that the entrepreneur is a person who, upon seeing a $10 bill in front of him, is alert to the opportunity and quickly grabs it. The alert person will seize it rapidly; the less alert will take longer to recognize the opportunity and to act on it. Not all entrepreneurs are created equal. By stressing alertness in this fashion, Kirzner emphasizes the quality of perception, perceiving an opportunity that is a sure thing; whereas in reality every profit opportunity is uncertain. Kirzner's best known case for illustrating alertness is that of the arbitrageur, the person who discovers the opportunity to buy at low prices and sell the same items at high prices, because of differences in intertemporal or interspatial demands. In these cases, Kirzner's entrepreneur requires neither capital, as per Mises's entrepreneur, nor imagination, as per Shackle's enterpriser.

In a series of unpublished papers, Lawrence White (1976), Robert Hébert (1980), and Murray Rothbard (1980) have identified shortcomings in the idea of the entrepreneur as merely the alert arbitrageur. The major difficulty identified with Kirzner's formulation is that it does not distinguish between arbitrageurship and uncertainty bearing. Arbitrage deals with present, known opportunities to exploit price differences that exceed transactions-transfer costs over time or space. Uncertainty, however, exists solely with respect to the future. Thus, by confining entrepreneurial activity to the practice of arbitrage, Kirzner downplays the importance of uncertainty in human decision making. The consequences are not trivial insofar as economic theory is concerned. By ignoring uncertainty and denying risk, Kirzner's theory cannot explain entrepreneurial losses, only entrepreneurial gains.*

Recently Kirzner (1981) has attempted to answer these criticisms while achieving a reconciliation between seemingly conflicting views. It now turns out that the entrepreneur-as-arbitrageur idea applies only to single-period market decisions (that is, discovery of past error), whereas multiperiod market decisions require the imagination and creativity of the Shacklean enterpriser. In this newest exposition Kirzner admits that uncertainty is central to the notion of entrepreneurial activity, but he claims that the relationship is more subtle than formerly supposed. It is claimed that entrepreneurial activity arises from present uncertainty about the unknowable future as well as from the discovery of past error that previously masked profit opportunities. Both views define profit opportunities, but the former gives wider scope to the framework-constructing talents of the entrepreneur and therefore emphasizes his history-making role. By comparison, the latter requires calculation and judgment within a given framework.

In essence, therefore, Kirzner now defends a synthetic view that combines the epoch-making activities of the entrepreneur

---

*Rothbard pointed out that even the arbitrageur is subject to uncertainty: "The arbitrageur can perceive that a product sells for one price at one place and at a higher price somewhere else, and therefore buy in the first place to sell in the second. But he better be cautious. The transactions are not instantaneous, and something might occur in the interim to change the seemingly certain profits into losses. It is, after all, possible that the other entrepreneurs, far from purblind to the profit opportunity lying await for arbitrage, knew something which our would-be arbitrageur does not" (1980, p. 3).

(a la Shackle) with the corrective adjustments of the arbitrageur, which he formerly stressed. For Kirzner, time and uncertainty merely modify the way in which the function of entrepreneurship is exercised, not the formal function itself. Thus one must specify the nature of the market process in order to understand the concrete manifestation of the entrepreneurial function. According to Kirzner

> In the single-period case alertness can at best discover hitherto overlooked current facts. In the multiperiod case entrepreneurial alertness must include the entrepreneur's perception of the way in which creative and imaginative action may vitally shape the kind of transactions that will be entered into in future market periods. (1981, p. 30)

It remains to be seen whether this attempted reconciliation will satisfy Kirzner's critics. It is noteworthy, however, that the peculiar gestalt of Kirzner's approach to entrepreneurship is reminiscent of A. P. Usher's (1954, 1955) characterization of invention. Usher hypothesized four steps in the inventive process, steps that constitute a "cumulative synthesis" approach. First, someone must recognize a problem or "unsatisfactory pattern" – a disequilibrium. The next two steps involve a collection of means to solve the problem and a final "act of insight" from which the solution emerges. Finally, a "critical revision" occurs during which the solution is implemented – a new equilibrium.*

At least one study has given partial corroboration to Kirzner's view of the entrepreneur. Patricia Braden (1977) concluded that the life histories of entrepreneurs in the state of Michigan demonstrated that their talents rested not on their managerial abilities but on their capacities to recognize opportunities, that is, their alertness. Still, because of its analytic asymmetry (that is, inability to explain losses), Kirzner's

---

*Following Usher, Frederick Rossini and Barry Bozeman define innovation as "mankind's striking response to the conjunction of resources and knowledge. [Innovation] is not only the seizing of emergent opportunities, but also a uniquely human response to perceived needs" (1977, p. 81).

formulation remains suspect among many economists, including other neo-Austrians. It remains to be seen whether Kirzner's latest exposition will change the form or the intensity of the debate.

Finally, a comparison between Kirzner's and Schumpeter's theories is instructive. Superficially, the Kirznerian entrepreneur appears to be the antithesis of the Schumpeterian entrepreneur, but fundamentally their differences are more apparent than real. A major distinction of Kirzner's theory is presumably that his entrepreneur is "an equilibrating force in the economy, not the reverse" (1979a, p. 115). But this difference is mainly one of perspective. Schumpeter maintained that the impact of entrepreneurial action must always be assessed with regard to some previous or existing equilibrium. Because innovation brings change, this implies that a past or present equilibrium is disturbed by the innovation. Consequently, Schumpeter portrayed the entrepreneur-innovator as a disequilibrating force. He and Kirzner agree that in the wake of each disequilibration there begins a movement toward a new equilibrium. However, the role of Schumpeter's entrepreneur in the reequilibration process is never quite made clear. Kirzner's perspective is the future. His entrepreneur springs into action upon recognizing a disequilibrium situation. But what is not made clear in Kirzner's exposition is how the disequilibrium arises in the first place. In the context just described, Schumpeter's entrepreneur is active; Kirzner's is passive. Schumpeter's entrepreneur creates opportunities for development, whereas Kirzner's entrepreneur, by one admission, helps fulfill the "potential for economic development that society already possesses" (1979a, p. 115) but has not yet exploited for lack of information.* Viewed from this perspective, one vision seems to complement the other. Moreover, both theories deny that risk taking is essential to the entrepreneurial function.

---

*How Kirzner may choose to alter this idea in view of his recent exposition of the nature of entrepreneurship in the multiperiod market is not clear.

ENTREPRENEURSHIP AND X-INEFFICIENCY

Austrian economists like Kirzner offer a theoretical alternative to the general equilibrium paradigm of neoclassical economics. Their framework eschews the comparative-statics, perfect-markets vision of economic activity in favor of a system that emphasizes change, error, and imperfections in markets and in human decision making. Yet theirs is not the only challenge to the dominant paradigm, for we have seen that Clark, Schumpeter, and Shackle have all launched criticisms and alternative visions of the neoclassical framework that have met with some success. Another recent challenge that has come from outside the Austrian circle is the theory of X-efficiency devised by Harvey Leibenstein.

It is debatable whether entrepreneurship is central to Leibenstein's theory or incidental to it. What is clear is that the X-efficiency paradigm excludes precisely those aspects of the neoclassical framework that virtually eliminated the role of the entrepreneur. In a perfectly competitive world of general equilibrium, all participants are viewed as successful maximizers of utility and all firms are seen as producing efficiently. Leibenstein rejects this vision, substituting inefficiency as the norm. The market imperfections that account for X-inefficiency in Leibenstein's (1979) theory arise chiefly from organizational entropy, human inertia, incomplete contracts between economic agents, and conflicting agent-principal interests. In the X-inefficient world, firms do not necessarily maximize profits, nor do they always minimize costs. Obviously, one's view of what the entrepreneur does depends on his vision of the market. The X-inefficient world is one of persistent slack, which implies the existence of entrepreneurial opportunities. According to Leibenstein (1968), these opportunities fall into four categories: the connection of different markets, correction of market deficiencies (gap-filling), completion of inputs, and creation or extension of time-binding, input-transforming entities (that is, firms). But Leibenstein's entrepreneur must work hard to discover such opportunities. The existence of slack and the fact that not all inputs are marketed tend to obscure profit signals, so that they must be ferreted out. A world with as many market imperfections as Leibenstein's must nevertheless give as wide a scope for entrepreneurial activity as a perfectly competitive situation takes away from it.

Leibenstein emphasizes the input-completing function as the critical role of the entrepreneur. This involves filling gaps in the production process and overcoming obstacles to production. Leibenstein asserts that "there are both empty spaces and fuzzy areas between what is being bought, and what can be done for productive purposes with what is bought"* (1979, p. 134). The one input that is always missing in Leibenstein's view is motivation. He views individual effort as a variable in production, and because of this, denies the existence of a unique production function. This last fact adds a dimension of entrepreneurial uncertainty that is augmented by organizational entropy within the firm, which the entrepreneur must try to overcome. Despite multiple responsibilities, however, input completion is the chief task of the entrepreneur in Leibenstein's paradigm:

> Another way of looking at this matter is to say that the product space is not continuous. It is not so dense everywhere that every variety of product exists. Products come in discontinuous chunks, as it were, and not as individual characteristics or qualities. Hence the entrepreneur has to marshal enough of the missing or difficult to get inputs to produce an integrated collection of qualities. (1979, p. 135)

Leibenstein's vision leads to an open-ended theory of profits. In answer to the question what do entrepreneurs get, Leibenstein replies "whatever they can, or are clever enough to arrange to get." The X-inefficiency framework does not favor one theory of profit over another, it emphasizes a menu of contractual possibilities.

---

*Less hostile critics of Leibenstein maintain that the existence of "fuzzy areas" is characteristic of his theory as well, while more hostile antagonists question the very existence of the concept of X-inefficiency (for example, Stigler 1976).

> The nub of the matter is that the entrepreneur, as a consequence of his activities as an *input completer*, finds himself to be in a strategic position to work out (usually favorable) contracts, which determine in what form he is to receive his reward. . . . Some possibilities are the following: (1) He can become the residual claimant; or (2) he can be one of a group (for example, common stockholders) who are residual claimants; or (3) he can "forego" or sell his residual claimant reward and take a fixed share immediately of the capitalized value of the enterprise; or (4) he can appoint himself to a strategic managerial role in the enterprise so that he may receive both a wage and a share in the residual claims. (1979, p. 136)

Leibenstein's paradigm seems to touch the Austrian framework at a number of critical junctures, yet Austrian theorists have remained somewhat skeptical of its analytical potency. The tendency is for Austrians to interpret Leibenstein's entrepreneurship as merely one interesting feature of the economic landscape, not as a factor central to the economic process. Kirzner has remarked that Leibenstein's entrepreneurship "is a feature that indeed seems to come into focus when observed through the X-efficiency lens; but the X-efficiency paradigm can be presented without any special reference to entrepreneurs" (1979b, p. 142). By contrast, in the Austrian framework, the entrepreneurial role is the key to understanding the entire course of economic phenomena. It is through the entrepreneur's thoughts and actions that what happens in the disequilibrium state is made intelligible.

THE HUMAN CAPITAL APPROACH

The next logical extension of the main lines of the arguments presented in this chapter was made by Nobel laureate T. W. Schultz. Schultz (1975) perceived in contemporary economic literature, including Kirzner's contribution, a failure to see the rewards that accrue to those who bring about the equilibrating process, especially as that process extends itself into nonmarket activities. In particular, Schultz sees entrepreneurship as a significant element in the human capital approach to understanding both market and nonmarket activities. He found the standard concept and treatment of entrepreneurs inadequate to this purpose for four reasons (1975, p. 832): the concept is restricted to businessmen, it does not take into account the differences in allocative abilities among entrepreneurs, the supply of entrepreneurship is not treated as a scarce resource, and there is no need for entrepreneurship in general equilibrium theory. It should be emphasized that these shortcomings are not to be found in Cantillon's original treatment, especially if one adopts a nontechnical definition of general equilibrium theory. But Schultz is on firm ground, at least, in asserting that the allocative abilities among entrepreneurs have seldom been the subject of close scrutiny in economics.

In this regard Schultz's contribution consists of two major advances: He redefined the concept of entrepreneurship as "the ability to deal with disequilibria," extending the notion to nonmarket activity (for example, household decisions, allocation of time), as well as market activity; and he brought evidence to bear on the effects of education on people's ability to perceive and react to disequilibria.* Part of his refinement, moreover, has been a reaffirmation of equilibration models. According to Schultz

> Unless we develop equilibrating models, the function of this particular ability cannot be analyzed. Within such models, the function of entrepreneurship would be much extended and the supply of entrepreneurial ability would be treated as a scarce resource. (1975, p. 843)

Like Kirzner, Schultz has turned away from the Schumpeterian paradigm in his attempt to redirect entrepreneurial theory. Schultz (1980) admits that Schumpeter succeeded in integrating the dynamics of technology and business enterprise, but he also underscores the fact that Schumpeter could not

---

*Edward Roberts and Herbert Wainer (1971) have examined other characteristics of entrepreneurs from a behavioralist perspective and their findings seem to complement Schultz's in regard to the effects of education. Specifically, they contend that an individual's home and religious background have strong influences on his goal orientation and motivation.

have anticipated the growth of research and development in the public sector. As a result of this growth, Schumpeter's entrepreneurs have become a decreasing part of the technological story.

One noteworthy aspect of the human capital approach is that it rejects the idea that the economic value of entrepreneurial activity is to be viewed as a return to risk bearing. While affirming the omnipresent nature of risk in a dynamic economy, Schultz nevertheless maintains that "the bearing of risk is not a unique attribute of entrepreneurs. Whereas entrepreneurs assume risk, there also are people who are not entrepreneurs who assume risk" (1980, p. 441). As it goes, this is a valid assertion, but it does not adequately address Kanbur's (1980) point that there is a kind of risk that is peculiar to the entrepreneurial function (see Chapter 7).

Fundamentally, Schultz takes the Mangoldt-Marshall position that the value of entrepreneurial action is a differential return to ability. His position is neatly summarized in the following passage:

> The substance of my argument is that disequilibria are inevitable in [a] dynamic economy. These disequilibria cannot be eliminated by law, by public policy, and surely not by rhetoric. A modern dynamic economy would fall apart were it not for the entrepreneurial actions of a wide array of human agents who reallocate their resources and thereby bring their part of the economy back into equilibrium. Every entrepreneurial decision to reallocate resources entails risk. What entrepreneurs do has an economic value. This value accrues to them as a rent, i.e., a rent which is a reward for their entrepreneurial performance. This reward is *earned*. Although this reward for the entrepreneurship of most human agents is small, in the aggregate in a dynamic economy it accounts for a substantial part of the increases in national income. The concealment of this part in the growth of national income implies that entrepreneurs have not received their due in economics. (1980, p. 443)

Schultz suggests that education is one determinant of people's ability to exercise entrepreneurial talent. Perception and alertness, however, may have other sources besides formal education. Fritz Machlup (1980) argues that formal education is only one form of knowledge; knowledge is also gained experientially and at different rates by different individuals. Individuals can accrue knowledge from their day-to-day experiences, which "will normally induce reflection, interpretations, discoveries, and generalizations . . ." (Machlup 1980, p. 179). More specifically, Machlup argues:

> Some alert and quick-minded persons, by keeping their eyes and ears open for new facts and theories, discoveries and opportunities, perceive what normal people of lesser alertness and perceptiveness, would fail to notice. Hence, new knowledge is available at little or no cost to those who are on the lookout, full of curiosity, and bright enough not to miss their chances. (1980, p. 179)

Should we synthesize Schultz and Machlup to conclude that entrepreneurial abilities stem from cognitive and experiential events? Investments in factual knowledge are clearly possible, but there may yet remain innate differences in individual capacities to receive and assimilate knowledge from their surroundings. If so, the human capital approach to entrepreneurship may ultimately rest on a genetic base.

CHAPTER 9

PAST, PRESENT,
AND FUTURE

The future belongs to the entrepreneurs.

Anonymous

The stated purpose at the outset of this volume was to explore the relationship between entrepreneurship and economic activity. Our approach has been historical and exegetic. Throughout, our chief concern has been with those economic writers who in some way advanced the theory of entrepreneurship, not merely with those who recognized the existence and function of the entrepreneur. Not surprisingly, our trace of history reveals that some of the issues involved in the economics of entrepreneurship have been resolved whereas others have not. In contemporary thought the entrepreneur is generally recognized as an independent factor of production along with land, labor, and capital. The distinction between manager and entrepreneur has also been firmly drawn. However, the ultimate place of risk and uncertainty in the theory of entrepreneurship is yet to be settled, as is the relationship between entrepreneurial activity and economic progress.

HOW MANY THEORIES?

One of the major difficulties confronting any investigation into the connection between entrepreneurship and economic activity is that in the broad expanse of time the entrepreneur has worn many faces and played many roles. There is as yet no consensus among economists regarding who the entrepreneur is and what he does. In an age when government policy seems to be taking a conscious turn toward alteration of incentives so as to encourage higher entrepreneurial activity, this lack of consensus presents more than an academic dilemma. Unless economists and policymakers can agree on the entrepreneur's identity and function, government policy aimed at enlarging the production controlled by entrepreneurial decisions cannot be fully informed. For example, if it turns out that Knightian uncertainty is a critical aspect of entrepreneurship, then it must also be recognized that unanticipated changes in government policies affecting business will enhance the uncertainty that entrepreneurs must face while fulfilling their economic function.

Unfortunately, as we can now appreciate, the historical record on the nature and role of the entrepreneur in the economy is ambiguous. Our review provides at least partial justification for a variety of concepts that we have summarized below, parenthetically noting those writers associated with each idea.

1. The entrepreneur is the person who assumes the risk associated with uncertainty (Cantillon, Thünen, Mangoldt, Mill, Hawley, Knight, Mises, Cole, Shackle).

2. The entrepreneur is a supplier of financial capital (Smith, Turgot, Ricardo, Böhm-Bawerk, Edgeworth, Pigou, Mises).

3. The entrepreneur is an innovator (Baudeau, Bentham, Thünen, Schmöller, Sombart, Weber, Schumpeter).

4. The entrepreneur is a decision maker (Cantillon, Menger, Marshall, Wieser, Walker, Keynes, Mises, Shackle, Cole, Kirzner, Schultz).

5. The entrepreneur is an industrial leader (Say, Walker, Marshall, Wieser, Sombart, Weber, Schumpeter).

6. The entrepreneur is a manager or superintendent (Say, Mill, Marshall, Menger).

7. The entrepreneur is an organizer or coordinator of economic resources (Wieser, Schmöller, Sombart, Weber, Clark, Schumpeter).

8. The entrepreneur is a proprietor of an enterprise (Wieser, Pigou).

9. The entrepreneur is an employer of factors of production (Walker, Keynes, Wieser).

10. The entrepreneur is a contractor (Bentham).

11. The entrepreneur is an arbitrageur (Cantillon, Kirzner).

12. The entrepreneur is the person who allocates resources to alternative uses (Kirzner, Schultz).

Some of these concepts clearly overlap; a dozen viewpoints do not necessarily establish a dozen different theories. Moreover, the list is not intended to be exhaustive, merely illustrative of the many facets of entrepreneurship expressed in economic literature.

As a matter of taxonomy, a theory of entrepreneurship may be either static or dynamic, but as we pursue the meaning of these terms we soon come to realize that only the latter has any significant operational meaning. In a static world neither change nor uncertainty is present. The entrepreneur's role in such a state could therefore be no more than what is implied in items 2, 6, 8, or 9. At best, the entrepreneur is a passive element in a static society because his actions merely constitute repetitions of past procedures and techniques already learned and implemented. Only in a dynamic world does the entrepreneur become a robust figure. Such a framework gives scope for entrepreneurial actions implied by items 1, 3, 4, 5, 7, 10, 11, and 12.

If we limit the field to dynamic theories — or more appropriately to theories grounded in a process view of competition

— we can collapse the above list into four generic types of entrepreneurial theories. For simplicity we shall label these types A, B, C, and D. Type A theories stress uncertainty as the chief burden of the entrepreneur. Type B theories downplay uncertainty and stress innovation instead. Type C theories treat entrepreneurship as a combination of uncertainty bearing and either innovation or "special ability." Type D theories emphasize the perception of and adjustment to disequilibria, with uncertainty and innovation receiving minor attention or none at all.

From this field we can derive the following schematic alignment of influential writers on the subject of entrepreneurship:

Theory Type

A *"Pure"* *Uncertainty*	*B* *"Pure"* *Innovation*	*C* *Uncertainty and* *Ability/Innovation*	*D* *Perception and* *Adjustment*
Cantillon	Schmöller	Baudeau	Clark
Hawley	Sombart	Bentham	Kirzner
Knight	Weber	Thünen	Schultz
Mises	Schumpeter	Mangoldt	
Shackle		Cole	

Forcing individuals into rigid categories is useful for achieving certain taxonomic ends but should not be allowed to obscure their individual differences. Thus, although we have placed Shackle in the tradition of Cantillon as a Type A theorist, it is clear that Shackle does not share the conviction of other Type A theorists that the economy exhibits a continuously operative tendency toward equilibrium. Likewise, we included Cole in the Type C category even though he stands apart from the rest of that group by his acceptance of Schumpeter's view that the entrepreneur is a disequilibrating force. Probably the greatest homogeneity exists among Type B and Type D theorists. As a group, Type B theorists have treated the entrepreneur as a disequilibrating force, whereas Type D theorists have regarded him as an equilibrating mechanism. Ultimately, the "radicals" in the development of entrepreneurial theory have been Schumpeter, his predecessors in the German historical school, and Shackle. Schumpeter broke tradition by treating the entrepreneur as a disequilibrating force; Shackle went even farther by rejecting the equilibrium paradigm altogether. The rest of the lot have remained within the equilibrium tradition, regardless of what type of entrepreneurial theory they have espoused.

THE QUEST FOR COMMON GROUND

Amid the diversity implied by the above scheme of things lies some substantial common ground. From Cantillon to Schultz, all of the theories of entrepreneurship reviewed in this volume have regarded the primary motives to productive activity as individualistic rather than social. In addition, they all share a functional orientation. That is, they all start by attributing to the entrepreneur an essential function in the productive process, and they subsequently explain entrepreneurial rewards by the degree of success attained fulfilling that function. This is different from a purely proprietary claim on income by virtue of mere asset ownership. Furthermore, the functional approach does not require the entrepreneur to be a member of a certain economic or social class.

All of the writers whose theories were reviewed in the preceding chapters believed that the entrepreneurial function, however they defined it, was an essential function in a capitalist society. How analogous functions might be carried out in a different society is altogether another question, one that we have not addressed in this work. This does not imply that entrepreneurship is absent from other societies, only that conclusions drawn from the study of human behavior under one set of institutional constraints are not necessarily applicable to a society operating under different institutional rules. By one definition the entrepreneur is merely a "rent seeker," and there are most assuredly "rent seekers" in the Soviet Union and its satellites just as there are in North America and Western Europe. It is difficult to invest such an indiscriminate entrepreneur with a specific function, however, so that he must ultimately exist apart from the field we now have under consideration.

Economists generally display a strong proclivity for functional theories, perhaps because they are heuristically more satisfactory than alternative approaches. But a functional theory may not capture all of the entrepreneurial gains or losses known to business practice. Schumpeter (1954, pp. 896-97) cited two possible reasons for this: In the first place, the entrepreneur who stands between the commodity and factor markets is better placed to exploit favorable situations — to capture certain "leftovers" or residuals. In the second place, whatever their nature in other respects, entrepreneurs' gains will practically always bear some relation to monopolistic pricing. We find the first of these arguments more compelling than the second, especially in view of Kirzner's (1973) attempt to clarify the distinction between competition and monopoly. By Kirzner's reasoning, true entrepreneurial gains have nothing to do with monopoly in its "proper" sense, which implies only that entry barriers exist. The problem of who has a legitimate claim to economic "leftovers" is, however, a thorny one that will, in our opinion, continue to plague the theory of entrepreneurship for some time to come.

TOWARD A SYNTHESIS

When we reflect on the fact that practically all past theories of entrepreneurship have centered either on uncertainty, innovation, or some combination of the two, it becomes incumbent upon us to recognize that uncertainty is a consequence of change whereas innovation is primarily a cause of change.* Thus, once we accept the fact of change, we must thereby expect entrepreneurship to have two faces — one that reveals itself when the level of inquiry deals with an explanation of change, the other when investigation concerns itself with the

---

*We do not deny that new methods and techniques themselves have consequences and that one of these consequences may be further innovation. Still, this does not deny the validity or relevance of the proposition we have stated.

effects of change. Despite the apparent simplicity of this point, it is one that has never been made explicit throughout the rather lengthy intellectual history of entrepreneurial theory. Were it otherwise, it seems unlikely that so many rival theories could have vied with each other so long for center stage.

An illustration of what we are talking about concerns one of the earliest stumbling blocks in the path of analytic advance on the subject, namely, the apparent inability or unwillingness of early writers to separate the role of entrepreneur from that of capitalist. True entrepreneurial gains, of course, have no definite relation to the size of the capital involved in enterprise, but one thing that capitalist and entrepreneur have in common is that an element of risk attends their actions. In the classical era, this commonality overshadowed small differences that, to the classical mind, were merely superficial. The chief social problem perceived by the classical economists was how to encourage the formation of capital that would be readily placed at the service of increased production. The last part of the preceding sentence is the crucial one. Certainly there were "capitalists" — those who accumulated wealth — in a feudal society, but they were not the merchant capitalists who rose to prominence in the seventeenth, eighteenth, and nineteenth centuries. These earlier "capitalists" were the landed aristocracy, whose capital was not "risked" in the production and sale of goods as is the common and pervasive practice of a market system.* The "new" capitalists of Adam Smith's day were those adventuresome people who took on large business risks in the hope of reaping great profits, and their presence and central importance in society made recognition of a second group of risk takers (that is, entrepreneurs) superfluous. Capital having been accumulated in the right hands, it was assumed that production would be organized and superintended by the selfsame person, and it was not deemed likely that the owner of capital would willingly give up its control and supervision; nor were there institutional factors encouraging him to do so

---

*We noted in Chapter 3 that Cantillon excluded this group of people from his class of "entrepreneurs," claiming that they did not "live at uncertainty."

until a later time. If this view seems shortsighted today, it is more the result of over 200 years of change in business practice than of a deficiency in the thought processes of our economic forebears. The fact is that at the same time that the term entrepreneur was evolving into more specialized use, so was the term capitalist, and for a time, at least, both meanings ran in the same channel.

The development just described may have persisted much longer had the focus of economic inquiry not switched dramatically from economic growth to income distribution. When emphasis shifted to the rewards for individual economic effort, the differences between capitalist and entrepreneur came into bold relief. It was then that perception, ingenuity, and judgment could be seen more clearly as characteristics separable from the accumulation and productive use of capital. But this breakthrough at one level created an impediment at another. The theory of income distribution operates largely within a static framework that does not give full scope to the actions of the entrepreneur. Therefore, a perspective that effectively highlighted the differences of the capitalist and the entrepreneur simultaneously suppressed the role of the entrepreneur as a force of change. This predicament is no less true of contemporary economics, where a thorough integration of the theories of growth and distribution has yet to be accomplished. Thus we are left with the fact that one's particular view of the entrepreneur is influenced by whether one is trying to develop a theory of growth or a theory of distribution.

Even within a theory of growth that gives wide berth to the role of the entrepreneur, however, a kind of integration is required to bring together causes and consequences so that the entrepreneurial role is displayed in all of its vital facets. In a dynamic context it seems as appropriate for Schumpeter to attribute "creative destruction" to the innovator/entrepreneur as it does for Kirzner or Schultz to outline the "entrepreneurial response" to a disequilibrium situation. The former view places the initiative for change on the entrepreneur, whereas the latter makes adjustment to change his specific task. The first notion seems narrow in that it does not give prominence to the element of uncertainty introduced by the unanticipated effects of any change — effects that may, incidentally, impact upon the fortune of the innovator responsible for the "creative destruction." The second idea is also deficient in that it is incapable of explaining how change occurs in the first place. Each theory is equipped to explain something the other is not. The question is whether there is room in economics for a theory that can explain both kinds of phenomena. Short of this kind of integration, history tells us that consensus on the nature and role of the entrepreneur will be long in coming.

IN SEARCH OF THE HEFFALUMP

Our historical review of the nature and role of the entrepreneur has come to an end. How far it has advanced understanding of the subject must remain problematic. Our research has provided few definitive answers to the tough questions that plague this area of economic discourse. Yet we hope that it has illuminated, however faintly, some of the dark corners of the subject. Historical perspective is very often the ground swell from which genuine analytic progress emanates. If this volume becomes a useful manual on the conceptual history of entrepreneurship, it will have been a fruitful endeavor.

Despite our best intentions, the entrepreneur remains an elusive figure. A decade ago, Peter Kilby borrowed from *Winnie-the-Pooh* to construct the following analogy:

> The search for the source of dynamic entrepreneurial performance has much in common with hunting the Heffalump. The Heffalump is a large and rather important animal. He has been hunted by many individuals using various ingenious trapping devices, but no one so far has succeeded in capturing him. All who claim to have caught sight of him report that he is enormous, but they disagree on his particularities. Not having explored his current habitat with sufficient care, some hunters have used as bait their own favorite dishes and have then tried to persuade people that what they caught was a Heffalump. However, very few are convinced, and the search goes on. (1971, p. 1)

As in the case of the Heffalump, the search for the true nature and function of the entrepreneur will undoubtedly continue long after the ink is dry on these pages. If our research has contributed in some small way to the stock of intellectual capital on the subject, then at least the search may henceforth proceed over new ground rather than trodden soil.

BIBLIOGRAPHY

Aitken, Hugh G. J. 1949. "The Analysis of Decisions." *Explorations in Entrepreneurial History* 1: 17-23.

Aristotle. 1924. "The Politics," translated by B. Jowett. In *Early Economic Thought*, edited by A. E. Monroe, pp. 3-29. Cambridge, Mass.: Harvard University Press.

Baudeau, Nicolas. 1910 [originally 1767]. *Premiere introduction a la philosophie économique*, edited by A. Dubois. Paris.

Bentham, Jeremy. 1952. *Jeremy Bentham's Economic Writings*, edited by W. Stark. London: Allen & Unwin.

_____. 1962 [originally 1838-43]. *The Works of Jeremy Bentham*, edited by John Bowring. New York: Russell & Russell.

Braden, Patricia L. 1977. *Technological Entrepreneurship*. Ann Arbor: Division of Research, University of Michigan.

Bronowski, Jacob. 1973. *The Ascent of Man*. Boston: Little, Brown.

Cantillon, Richard. 1931. *Essai sur la nature du commerce en général*, edited and translated by H. Higgs. London: Macmillan.

Carlin, Edward A. 1956. "Schumpeter's Constructed Type — The Entrepreneur." *Kyklos* 9: 27-43.

Clark, John Bates. 1892. "Insurance and Business Profits." *Quarterly Journal of Economics* 7: 45-54.

_____. 1899. *The Distribution of Wealth*. London: Macmillan.

_____. 1907. *Essentials of Economic Theory*. New York: Macmillan.

117

Cochran, Thomas C. 1968. "Entrepreneurship." *International Encyclopedia of the Social Sciences*, pp. 87-91.

Cole, Arthur H. 1946. "An Approach to the Study of Entrepreneurship: A Tribute to Edwin F. Gay." *Journal of Economic History* 6: 1-15.

_____. 1949. "Entrepreneurship and Entrepreneurial History." In *Change and the Entrepreneur*, prepared by the Research Center in Entrepreneurial History, pp. 85-107. Cambridge, Mass.: Harvard University Press.

_____. 1959. *Business Enterprise in Its Social Setting*. Cambridge, Mass.: Harvard University Press.

Davenport, H. J. 1913. *Economics of Enterprise*. New York: Macmillan.

de Roover, Raymond. 1963a. "The Organization of Trade." In *The Cambridge Economic History of Europe* III: 49-50.

_____. 1963b. "The Scholastic Attitude Toward Trade and Entrepreneurship." *Explorations in Entrepreneurial History* 3: 76-87.

Deutsch, Karl W. 1949. "A Note on the History of Entrepreneurship, Innovation and Decision-Making." *Explorations in Entrepreneurial History* 1: 8-12.

Dobb, Maurice, 1937. "Entrepreneur." *Encyclopedia of the Social Sciences*, pp. 558-60.

Dorfman, Joseph. 1959. *The Economic Mind in American Civilization*. New York: Viking Press.

Edgeworth, Francis Y. 1904. "The Theory of Distribution." *Quarterly Journal of Economics* 18: 159-219.

_____. 1925. "Application of the Differential Calculus to Economics." In *Papers Relating to Political Economy*, pp. 367-82. New York: Burt Franklin.

Evans, George H., Jr. 1949. "The Entrepreneur and Economic Theory: An Historical and Analytical Approach." *American Economic Review* 39: 336-55.

Forrester, Jay W. 1965. "A New Corporate Design." *Industrial Management Review* 7: 5-18.

Gay, Edwin F. 1923-24. "The Rhythm of History." *Harvard Graduates' Magazine* 32: 1-16.

Halévy, Elie. 1955. *The Growth of Philosophic Radicalism*, translated by Mary Morris. Boston: Beacon Press.

Harbison, Frederick. 1956. "Entrepreneurial Organization as a Factor in Economic Development." *Quarterly Journal of Economics* 70: 364-79.

Hawley, F. B. 1892. "The Fundamental Error of *Kapital und Kapitalzins.*" *Quarterly Journal of Economics* 6: 280-307.

_____. 1893. "The Risk Theory of Profit." *Quarterly Journal of Economics* 7: 459-79.

_____. 1900. "Enterprise and Profit." *Quarterly Journal of Economics* 15: 75-105.

Hébert, R. F. 1980. "Was Richard Cantillon an Austrian Economist?" Paper presented at the Liberty Fund Symposium on Richard Cantillon, Asilomar, Calif.

Hennings, K. H. 1980. "The Transition from Classical to Neoclassical Economic Theory: Hans von Mangoldt." *Kyklos* 33: 658-82.

Hirschman, Albert O. 1958. *The Strategy of Economic Development*. New Haven, Conn.: Yale University Press.

Hoselitz, Bert F. 1960. "The Early History of Entrepreneurial Theory." In *Essays in Economic Thought: Aristotle to Marshall*, edited by J. J. Spengler and W. R. Allen, pp. 234-58. Chicago: Rand McNally.

Hutchison, T. W. 1953. *A Review of Economic Doctrines, 1870-1929*. Oxford: Clarendon Press.

Jenks, Leland H. 1949. "Role Structure of Entrepreneurial Personality." In *Change and the Entrepreneur*, prepared by the Research Center in Entrepreneurial History, pp. 108-52. Cambridge, Mass.: Harvard University Press.

Jevons, William S. 1931 [originally 1881]. "Richard Cantillon and the Nationality of Political Economy." Reprinted in *Essai sur la nature du commerce en général*, by Richard Cantillon, edited by H. Higgs. London: Macmillan.

Kanbur, S. M. 1979. "Of Risk Taking and the Personal Distribution of Income." *Journal of Political Economy* 87: 769-97.

———. 1980. "A Note on Risk Taking, Entrepreneurship, and Schumpeter." *History of Political Economy* 12: 489-98.

Keynes, John Maynard. 1964. *The General Theory of Employment, Interest, and Money*. New York: Harcourt, Brace and World.

Kihlstrom, Richard E., and Jean-Jacques Laffront. 1979. "A General Equilibrium Entrepreneurial Theory of Firm Formation Based on Risk Aversion." *Journal of Political Economy* 89: 719-48.

Kilby, Peter. 1971. "Hunting the Heffalump." In *Entrepreneurship and Economic Development*, edited by Peter Kilby, pp. 1-40. New York: Free Press.

Kirzner, Israel M. 1973. *Competition & Entrepreneurship*. Chicago: University of Chicago Press.

———. 1979a. *Perception, Opportunity, and Profit: Studies in the Theory of Entrepreneurship*. Chicago: University of Chicago Press.

———. 1979b. "Comment: X-Inefficiency, Error, and the Scope for Entrepreneurship." In *Time, Uncertainty and Disequilibrium*, edited by Mario Rizzo. Lexington, Mass.: Heath.

———. 1981. "Uncertainty, Discovery and Human Action." Paper presented at the New York University-Liberty Fund Centenary Conference on Ludwig von Mises, New York.

Knight, Frank H. 1921. *Risk, Uncertainty and Profit*. New York: Houghton Mifflin.

———. 1942. "Profits and Entrepreneurial Functions." *Journal of Economic History* 2: 126-32.

_____ . 1951. *The Economic Organization*. New York: Augustus M. Kelley.

Koestler, Arthur. 1959. *The Sleepwalkers*. London: Macmillan.

Kuhn, W. E. 1970. *The Evolution of Economic Thought*. Cincinnati: South-Western.

Leibenstein, H. 1968. "Entrepreneurship and Development." *American Economic Review* 48: 72-83.

_____ . 1979. "The General X-Efficiency Paradigm and the Role of the Entrepreneur." In *Time, Uncertainty and Disequilibrium*, edited by Mario Rizzo. Lexington, Mass.: Heath.

Macdonald, Ronan. 1971. "Schumpeter and Max Weber: Central Visions and Social Theories." In *Entrepreneurship and Economic Development*, edited by Peter Kilby, pp. 71-94. New York: Free Press.

Machlup, Fritz. 1980. *Knowledge and Knowledge Production*. Princeton, N. J.: Princeton University Press.

Maidique, Modesto A. 1980. "Entrepreneurs, Champions, and Technological Innovation." *Sloan Management Review* 21: 59-76.

Mangoldt, H. von. 1855. "The Precise Function of the Entrepreneur and the True Nature of Entrepreneur's Profit." In *Some Readings in Economics*, edited by F. M. Taylor, pp. 34-49. Ann Arbor, Mich.: George Wahr, 1907.

Marshall, Alfred. 1961. *Principles of Economics*. 9th ed. London: Macmillan.

Marshall, Alfred, and Mary Paley Marshall. 1886. *Economics of Industry*. London: Macmillan.

Martin, D. T. 1979. "Alternative Views of Mengerian Entrepreneurship." *History of Political Economy* 11: 271-85.

Meek, R. L. 1973. *Turgot on Progress, Sociology and Economics*. Cambridge: University Press.

Menger, Carl. 1950. *Principles of Economics*, translated by J. Dingwall and B. F. Hoselitz. Glencoe, Ill.: Free Press.

Mises, Ludwig von. 1949. *Human Action: A Treatise on Economics*. New Haven, Conn.: Yale University Press.

———. 1951. *Profit and Loss*. South Holland, Ill.: Consumers-Producers Economic Service.

Neale, W. C. 1957. "The Market in Theory and History." In *Trade and Market in the Early Empires*, edited by K. Polanyi et al. Chicago: Henry Regnery.

Papandreau, Andreas G. 1943. "The Location and Scope of the Entrepreneurial Function." Ph.D. dissertation, Harvard University.

Pigou, A. C. 1929. *Industrial Fluctuations*. 2d ed. London: Macmillan.

———. 1949. *Employment and Equilibrium*. 2d ed. London: Macmillan.

Quesnay, François. 1888. *Oeuvres economiques et philosophiques*, edited by A. Oncken. Paris and Frankfurt.

Redlich, Fritz. 1957. "Towards a Better Theory of Risk." *Explorations in Entrepreneurial History* 10: 33-39.

———. 1966. "Toward the Understanding of an Unfortunate Legacy." *Kyklos* 19: 709-16.

Roberts, Edward B., and Herbert A. Wainer. 1971. "Some Characteristics of Technical Entrepreneurs." *IEEE Transactions on Engineering Management* EM-18: 100-9.

Rossini, Frederick, and Barry Bozeman. 1977. "National Strategies for Technological Innovation." *Administration and Society* 9: 81-110.

Rothbard, Murray N. 1980. "Professor Hébert on Entrepreneurship." Paper presented at the Cantillon Tricentennial Conference, Liberty Fund and the Institute for Humane Studies, Asilomar, Calif.

Rothschild, M., and J. E. Stiglitz. 1976. "An Essay in the Economics of Imperfect Information." *Quarterly Journal of Economics* 90: 629-50.

Routh, Guy. 1975. *The Origin of Economic Ideas*. White Plains, N. Y.: International Arts and Science Press.

Sass, Stephen A. 1978. "Entrepreneurial Historians and History: An Essay in Organized Intellect." Ph.D. dissertation, Johns Hopkins University.

Say, J. B. 1840. *Cours complet d'economie politique pratique*. 2d ed. Paris.

_____. 1845. *A Treatise on Political Economy*. 4th ed., translated by C. R. Prinsep. Philadelphia: Grigg & Elliot.

Schon, Donald A. 1963. "Champions for Radical New Inventions." *Harvard Business Review* 2: 77-86.

_____. 1976. *Technology and Change: The New Heraclitus*. New York: Delacorte Press.

Schultz, Theodore W. 1975. "The Value of the Ability to Deal with Disequilibria." *Journal of Economic Literature* 13: 827-46.

_____. 1980. "Investment in Entrepreneurial Ability." *Scandinavian Journal of Economics* 82: 437-48.

Schumpeter, Joseph A. 1928. "The Instability of Capitalism." *Economic Journal* 38: 361-86.

_____. 1939. *Business Cycles*. New York: McGraw-Hill.

_____. 1947. "The Creative Response in Economic History." *Journal of Economic History* 7: 149-59.

_____. 1954. *History of Economic Analysis*, edited by E. B. Schumpeter. New York: Oxford University Press.

_____. 1961. *The Theory of Economic Development*. New York: Oxford University Press.

_____. 1965. "Economic Theory and Entrepreneurial History." In *Explorations in Enterprise*, edited by Hugh G. J. Aitken, pp. 45-64. Cambridge, Mass.: Harvard University Press.

Shackle, G. L. S. 1955. *Uncertainty in Economics*. Cambridge: University Press.

———. 1966. *The Nature of Economic Thought*. Cambridge: University Press.

———. 1974. *Keynesian Kaleidics*. Edinburgh: Edinburgh University Press.

Shove, G. F. 1942. "The Place of Marshall's 'Principles' in the Development of Economic Theory." *Economic Journal* 52: 294-329.

Smith, Adam. 1937. *The Wealth of Nations*. New York: Random House.

Souder, William E. 1981. "Encouraging Entrepreneurship in the Large Corporation." *Research Management* 24: 18-21.

Spengler, J. J. 1949. Discussion to "Possibilities for a Realistic Theory of Entrepreneurship." *American Economic Review* 39: 352-56.

———. 1959. "Adam Smith's Theory of Economic Growth – Part II." *Southern Economic Journal* 26: 1-12.

———. 1960. "Richard Cantillon: First of the Moderns." In *Essays in Economic Thought: Aristotle to Marshall*, edited by J. J. Spengler and W. R. Allen, pp. 105-40. Chicago: Rand McNally.

Spengler, J. J., and W. R. Allen, eds. 1960. *Essays in Economic Thought: Aristotle to Marshall*. Chicago: Rand McNally.

Stigler, G. J. 1976. "The Xistence of X-efficiency." *American Economic Review* 66: 213-16.

Strauss, James H. 1944. "The Entrepreneur: The Firm." *Journal of Political Economy* 52: 112-27.

Streissler, Erich. 1972. "To What Extent Was the Austrian School Marginalist?" *History of Political Economy* 4: 426-41.

Taussig, F. W. 1915. *Principles of Economics*, rev. ed., vol. II. New York: Macmillan.

Taymans, Adrien C. 1949. "George Tarde and Joseph A. Schumpeter: A Similar Vision." *Explorations in Entrepreneurial History* 1: 9-17.

Thünen, J. H. von. 1960. *The Isolated State in Relation to Agriculture and Political Economy*, vol. 2., translated by B. W. Dempsey. In *The Frontier Wage*, by B. W. Dempsey, pp. 187-368. Chicago: Loyola University Press.

Tuttle, Charles A. 1927. "The Entrepreneur Function in Economic Literature." *Journal of Political Economy* 35: 501-21.

Usher, A. P. 1954. *A History of Mechanical Inventions*. Cambridge, Mass.: Harvard University Press.

_____ . 1955. "Technical Change and Capital Formation." In *Capital Formation and Economic Growth*, pp. 523-50. New York: National Bureau of Economic Research.

Walker, Francis A. 1876. *The Wages Question*. New York: Henry Holt.

_____ . 1884. *Political Economy*. New York: Henry Holt.

Weber, Max. 1930. *The Protestant Ethic and the Spirit of Capitalism*, translated by Talcott Parsons. New York: Scribner's.

White, L. H. 1976. "Entrepreneurship, Imagination and the Question of Equilibration." Manuscript.

Wieser, Friedrich von. 1927. *Social Economics*, translated by A. F. Hindrichs. New York: Adelphi.

Zrinyi, Joseph. 1962. "Entrepreneurial Behavior in Economic Theory: An Historical and Analytical Approach." Ph.D. dissertation, Georgetown University.

INDEX OF NAMES

ABOUT THE AUTHOR

Robert F. Hébert is professor and head of the Economics Department at Auburn University. He is the coauthor, along with R. B. Ekelund, Jr., of a popular economics text entitled *A History of Economic Theory and Method* (New York: McGraw-Hill, 1975) and has lectured in the United States and abroad. His research and reviews have been published in *Quarterly Journal of Economics*, *Economica*, *Economic Inquiry*, *Southern Economic Journal*, *Journal of Public Economics*, and *History of Political Economy*, among others. Dr. Hébert holds a B.S., M.S., and Ph.D. in economics from Louisiana State University, Baton Rouge, Louisiana.

Albert N. Link is an associate professor of economics at Auburn University. He has published widely in the field of economics, especially in the areas of innovation and technological change. He is the author of *Research and Development Activity in U.S. Manufacturing* (New York: Praeger, 1981), and his research articles have appeared in such journals as the *American Economic Review*, *Journal of Political Economy*, *Journal of Industrial Economics*, and *Public Choice*.

Dr. Link holds a B.S. (1971) in mathematics from the University of Richmond and a Ph.D. (1976) in economics from Tulane University. He has been on the faculty at Auburn University since 1976; most recently he has been a visiting lecturer at the Maxwell School of Citizenship at Syracuse University.